IMAGES
of America

CHIMNEY ROCK AND
RUTHERFORD COUNTY

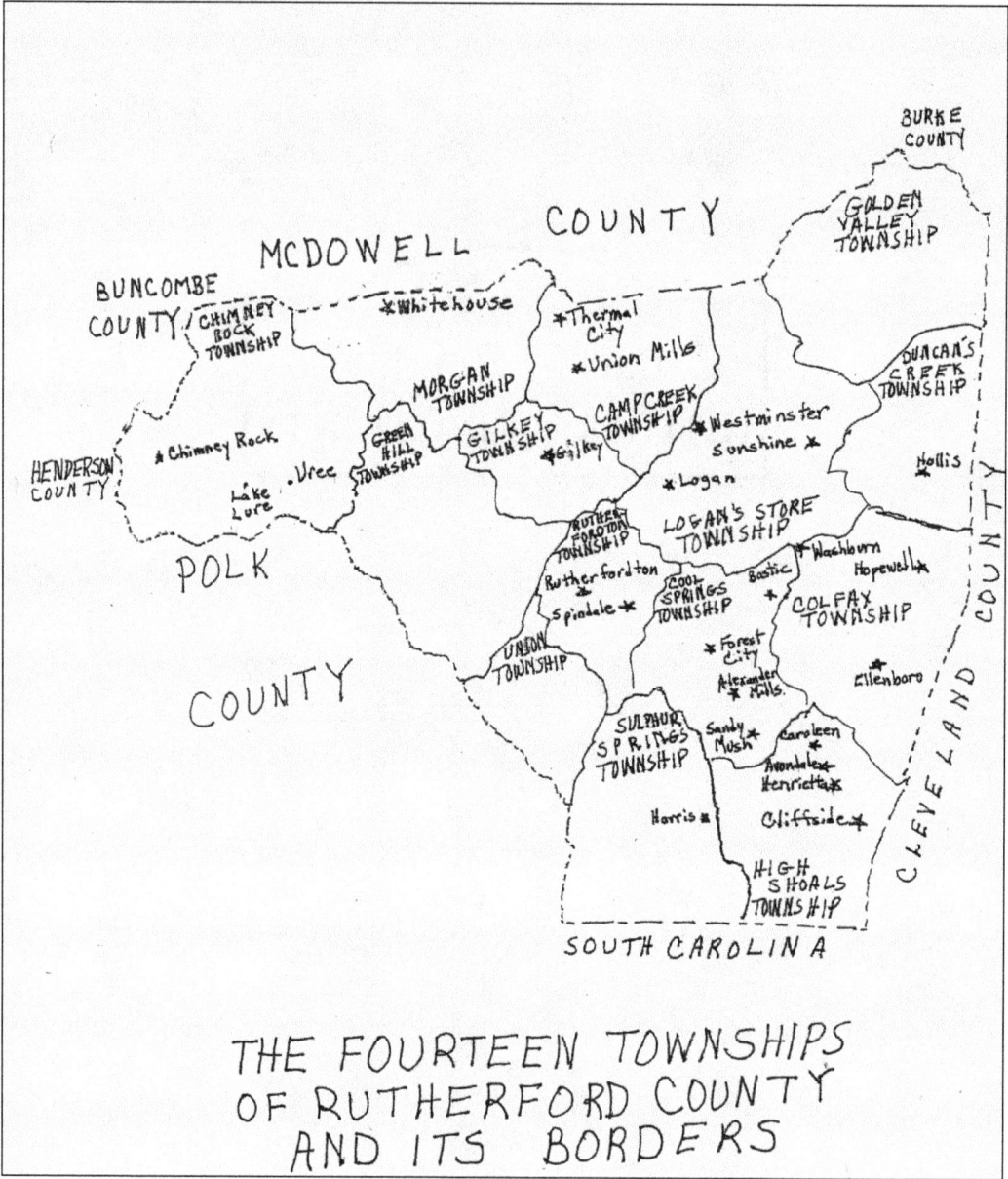

This image shows the 14 townships of Rutherford County.

IMAGES
of America

CHIMNEY ROCK AND RUTHERFORD COUNTY

Anita Price Davis and Barry E. Hambright

ARCADIA
PUBLISHING

Published by Arcadia Publishing
Charleston SC, Chicago IL, Portsmouth NH, San Francisco CA

Library of Congress Catalog Card Number: 2002112609

For all general information contact Arcadia Publishing at:
Telephone 843-853-2070
Fax 843-853-0044
E-mail sales@arcadiapublishing.com
For customer service and orders:
Toll-Free 1-888-313-2665

Visit us on the Internet at www.arcadiapublishing.com

While working on this book, Anita could hear her stepfather's voice naming the places he (an electrician) had worked—Puzzle Creek, Shingle Hollow, Golden Valley, Old Cove Road, Duncan's Creek, Sunshine. These places were instrumental in the development of the county and essential to an accurate depiction of the area. His love of history and his knowledge of geography were contagious, and Anita misses his wisdom immensely. This book is dedicated with love to Robert Ewart Burns.

4

CONTENTS

ACKNOWLEDGMENTS

This book is not the work of one person. Many people deserve credit. On each photograph or postcard, we have tried to identify the specific source. There are several additional contributors who have been particularly instrumental in the completion of this work.

W.H. McArthur generously gave his photographs and shared others that were a part of the legacy of his uncle, Will McArthur. McArthur e-mailed images, arranged for deliveries of disks at a dentist office, hunted for cornerstones on old buildings, furnished memories, traced down the names of artists, and welcomed Anita into his home on short notice. We are grateful to him and to his wife for their friendship and their encouragement.

James M. Walker (P.O. Box 24, Ellenboro NC 28040) was a treasure chest of knowledge, ideas, suggestions, and professionalism. His photographic expertise has enabled him to capture many images that were not available through other sources. His unfailing good humor and enthusiasm made his association on this project priceless. His superior mapping skills made trips about the county scenic and efficient.

The following organizations have helped on this project: the Reprint Company (Spartanburg), Liberty Press, Duke Energy Company, Chimney Rock Park, Grindstaff's Interiors, McKinney-Landreth Funeral Home, Esmeralda Inn, the Lake Lure Inn, the Post Mark Collectors Club, the Union Mills Fire Department, Isothermal Community College, Converse College, the American Legion, the VFW, and Gardner-Webb University. Thermal City Gold and Gem Mine contributed knowledge and pictures to the book. Steve Massengill of the North Carolina Office of Archives and History was, as always, efficient and interested.

The family of Raleigh Rutherford Haynes, who positively and richly impacted the entire county, shared unselfishly their knowledge, artifacts, and friendship. Particular thanks go to Mrs. Hazel Haynes Bridges for opening her home, her files, and her heart. We are grateful also to Anne and Paula Cargill, Mr. and Mrs. Grover C. Haynes Jr., and Mrs. Janice Swing.

Many people have showed support and interest through verbal encouragement and through donations of pictures, postcards, and information. Mr. and Mrs. Damon Huskey shared their family's keepsakes generously. Jerrell Bedford continues to give and encourage. Dr. Worth Bridges Jr. shared his memories and his photographs with us. Wanda Costner Robbins, Louise Hunt, and the Ruth Sunday School Class made suggestions and listened and listened and listened. Mr. and Mrs. Milton Robinson Jr. investigated and found information that no one else had discovered. Mary Thompson rejoiced with us in things remembered and gave us items that no one else could have had. Horton Landreth shared priceless photographs. Mr. and Mrs. Bill Robbins, Carolyn Grindstaff Barbee, Boyce Grindstaff, Walda Carpenter, Frances Gettys Bailey, Sara Daves, Roy Lewis McKain, Joyce McFarland, and Ellenboro Principal Frank Wall shared recollections, photographs, postcards, and support. James R. Brown, publisher of *The Daily Courier*, purchased rights to several local newspapers, including *The Forest City Courier*, *The Spindale Sun*, and *The Rutherford County News*; he gave us rights to use these papers and photographs in the volume. Jim Bishop of WCAB, Virginia Rucker of *The Daily Courier*, Mel at the Isothermal Bookstore, and Diane and Pete Dickerson of Fireside Books encourage and continue to publicize our work. Appreciation goes also to Frances Melton, Lucille Carpenter, Barbara and Bud Greene, Dan and Annette Martin, Linda and Charles Bridges, and Joann Bumgardner Bridges. Colleen Biggerstaff shared her dearest photographic memories with me.

We extend our thanks to our editor Laura New, our families, and our friends who accept us as we are and yet encourage us to become better. Most of all we thank Rutherford County for its confirmation of our work and of us; Rutherford County people are truly "small town friendly."

INTRODUCTION

Rutherford County lies in the piedmont region of North Carolina and at the border of North and South Carolina. Individuals who were not afraid of frontier living began its settlement in the 1700s. The large county unit of which present-day Rutherford County was a part carried the name Tryon County, a county created in 1769 by a 1768 act. The boundaries of Tryon County are not clear, but they appear to extend into the area inhabited by the Cherokee. Many of the settlers of this rural area professed their attachment and loyalty to the English government and proudly carried the name of Loyalists.

Rutherford County officially came into existence in April of 1779 as a result of the division of Tryon County into two separate counties: Lincoln and Rutherford. The name is a tribute to Brig. Gen. Griffith Rutherford who served in the Revolutionary War.

The South Carolina state line borders Rutherford County on the south; McDowell and Burke Counties form its northern border. Cleveland County is on the east. Henderson, Buncombe, and Polk Counties are on the west.

The county seat of Rutherford County is Rutherfordton, which once bore the name of Gilbert Town. Westward from Rutherfordton to the state capital, Raleigh, is about 216 miles.

In the late summer of 1780, Ferguson and his dragoons moved into Tryon County and camped at Gilbert Town, now Rutherfordton. Before the sun went down on October 7, 1780, Ferguson and 119 of his men would die at the Battle of Kings Mountain. An additional 664 would become prisoners; 123 more would suffer wounds. By October 14, 1780, the American Patriots who were moving their prisoners westward had reached Biggerstaff's Old Fields near Sunshine in Logan's Store Township. After a trial with a jury of 12 officers, the Patriots hanged nine Loyalists. When the Patriots received word that Tarlton would be at Gilbert Town by morning, they moved on—and left the bodies still hanging.

Residents of Rutherford County had many ways to earn a livelihood. Mining, lumbering, farming, tourism, milling, and retailing were particularly important to the county. By 1856 railroads began to find their niche in the county. In the late 1800s and early 1900s, manufacturing began to prosper throughout Rutherford County. Mills sprang up about the county in Cliffside, Henrietta, Avondale, Alexander Mills, Spindale, Rutherfordton, Forest City and Ellenboro. Villages close to the plants gave workers a choice of housing. Occupations, homes, and lifestyles of Rutherford County families began to change drastically.

The county was experiencing many other changes. The first banks in the county began to appear by 1891, and cars became more popular. Many residents saw their first car when Thomas Edison spent some time in the county looking for cobalt for storage batteries. By January 1, 1930, the Romina became the first theatre in the county with sound equipment. Ellenboro boasted the first telephone exchange in the county.

Rutherford County contains 14 townships. These divisions form the skeleton of this book. Townships are combined in some cases to give a total of eight chapters for the book. Each chapter contains a vast array of pictures and likenesses that depict the townships then and now.

A tour of Rutherford County through these photographs, captions, and postcard images reveals the area's diversity—the rural and the urban scene, the mountains and the foothills, the landmarks, the natural wonders, the churches, the schools and colleges, work and leisure-time activities, things old and new, and particularly the sites that are important enough to find inclusion in the National Register of Historic Places. Most importantly, the tour of Rutherford County through this volume will include a study of its people—the young and the old, the white-collar and the blue-collar workers, the rich and the poor, the workers and the unemployed, and the ethnically different. Missing, however, is a view of the large city because there is none in the county. The tour is also devoid of unwelcoming crowds and hostile neighborhoods. The traveler through this book and through an actual trip will find that Rutherford County does indeed live up to its nickname—Small Town Friendly. Relax and enjoy your trip. The images will tell it all.

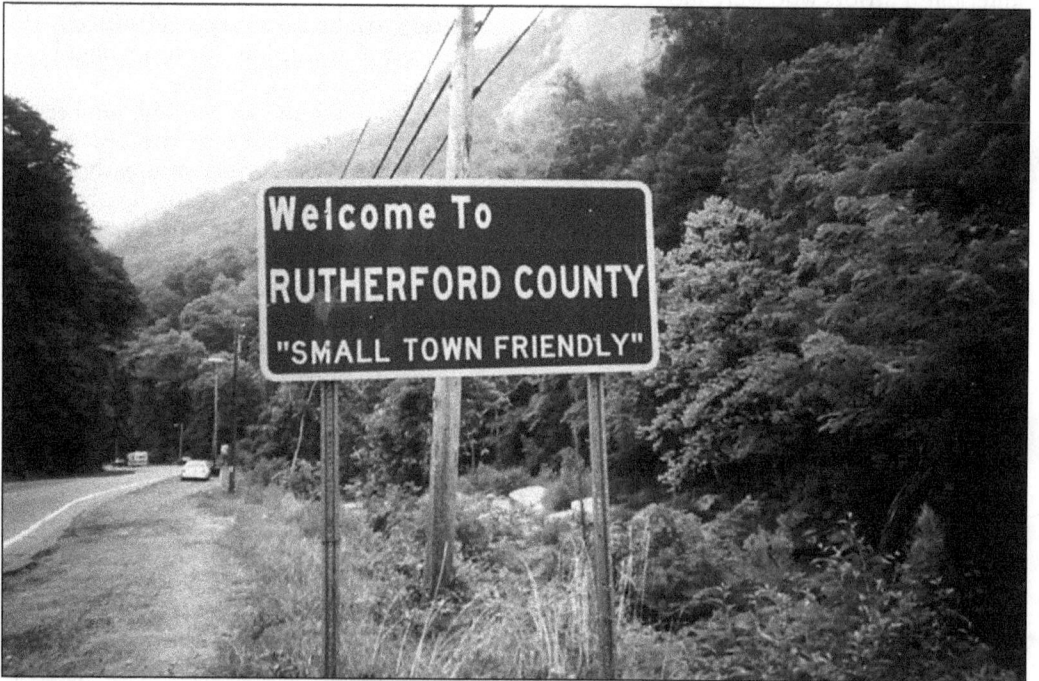

This sign at the entry into Rutherford County presents its slogan: Small Town Friendly.

One

CHIMNEY ROCK
TOWNSHIP

Chimney Rock Township is the most western of the townships of Rutherford County. McDowell County lies to the north and McDowell, Buncombe, and Henderson Counties form its westernmost edge. Morgan and Green Hill Townships border Chimney Rock Township to the east, and Polk County lies to the south. The township includes Lake Lure (established in 1925 and incorporated in 1927), a town on a lake of the same name; Chimney Rock, a resort community that was named for the granite monolith rising from Chimney Rock Mountain and whose post office has been in existence since 1843; Uree, a community on the Broad River; the Bottomless Pools, a popular natural feature and tourist attraction; Bills Creek community on the creek of the same name; much magnificent terrain; and many natural landmarks.

View from Top of Chimney Rock N. C.

This early view from the top of Chimney Rock does not reflect the later development of the area. (Raphael Tuck and Son, Postcard Series Number 2487, Hendersonville, North Carolina.)

Jerome Freeman bought Chimney Rock in 1880 from the Speculation Land Company. Guilford Nanney helped with the creation of the trail system in the park. After building a trail to the chimney and a stair to the top, Freeman opened Chimney Rock Park in 1885 to the public. (Raphael Tuck and Son, Postcard Series Number 2487, Hendersonville, North Carolina. Printed in Germany.)

The Opera Box, high upon the precipice overlooking Chimney Rock and Lake Lure, affords the traveler an unobstructed panorama on three sides. One may enjoy the scenery while resting on the comfortable benches. (Asheville Postcard Company, Asheville, North Carolina.)

On January 31, 1908, it became unlawful to transport alcohol in North Carolina. The state voted overwhelmingly against repealing Prohibition on November 7, 1933. However, making and transporting illegal liquor was a livelihood for some county residents, and the postcard above shows an 80-gallon moonshine still in the mountains. The most popular movie depicting the making and running of moonshine was a 1958 feature, *Thunder Road*, with Robert Mitchum. He frequented Chimney Rock and Lake Lure during the filming; Betty Bumgardner Conner served him at the Log Shop Restaurant in Lake Lure. (Information courtesy of Joann Bumgardner Bridges. Asheville Postcard Company, Asheville, North Carolina.)

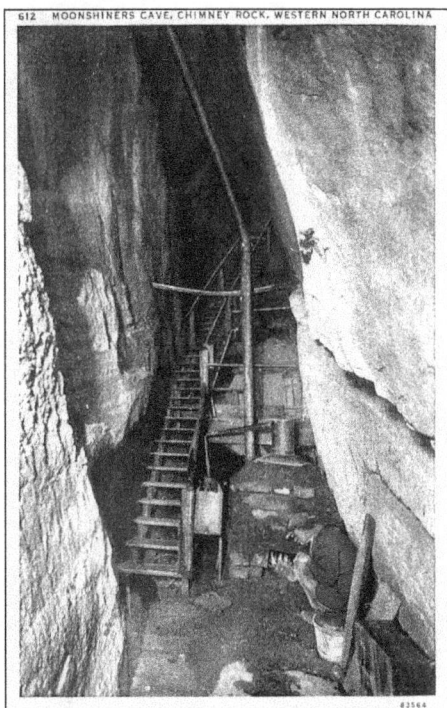

This postcard shows a moonshiner's cave with all of its associations. The caption describes it as a "weird experience for the visitor to Chimney Rock, North Carolina." Many caves lie within Chimney Rock Park. The caves in the park area are too cold for bats to use for hibernation, but some may rest inside during the summer. These caves are fissure caves and are different from the limestone caves such as Carlsbad Caverns. Limestone caves are the result of the dissolution of limestone by acid water. (Asheville Postcard Company, Asheville, North Carolina.)

536 - HICKORY NUT FALLS, NEAR CHIMNEY ROCK, NORTH CAROLINA

Hickory Nut Falls is a slender cascade that falls 400 feet down the cliffs of Chimney Rock Mountain. (Deuel News Company, Asheville, North Carolina.)

Dr. Lucius Morse contracted tuberculosis in 1899 and spent time recuperating in the mountains of North Carolina. He saw possibilities in the beautiful area, so he and his brothers bought Chimney Rock in 1904 and developed the property further. The early visitor to Chimney Rock would find Hickory Nut Falls was only a short walk from Chimney Rock on a path that Morse and brothers paid to have developed. Guilford Nanney, a local, was responsible for the first trail (now identified as the Cliff Trail), for the trail to the falls, and for the complicated stairways from the parking lot, around Pulpit Rock, and to the top of the chimney. (Asheville Postcard Company, Asheville, North Carolina.)

N-758   PATH TO HICKORY NUT FALLS, CHIMNEY ROCK MOUNTAIN, WESTERN NORTH CAROLINA

E-8040

Tom Turner built the Esmeralda Inn and opened it in 1892. The old Pony Express and Stagecoach Route over the mountains used it as a stopping point. As early as 1899 celebrities were frequenting the inn; Lew Wallace finished the script for his play *Ben Hur* in Room #9, and Clark Gable, Mary Pickford, Gloria Swanson, and Douglas Fairbanks also stayed here. After a fire in 1917, a new Esmeralda, shown above, was built on the original foundation. (Asheville Postcard Company, Asheville, North Carolina.)

This view of the Esmeralda shows the rock foundation and the three floors before a 1997 fire ravaged it. The newly rebuilt and restored Esmeralda on Highway 74-A is again a place for tired people seeking solitude and peace. (Asheville Postcard Company, Asheville, North Carolina.)

13

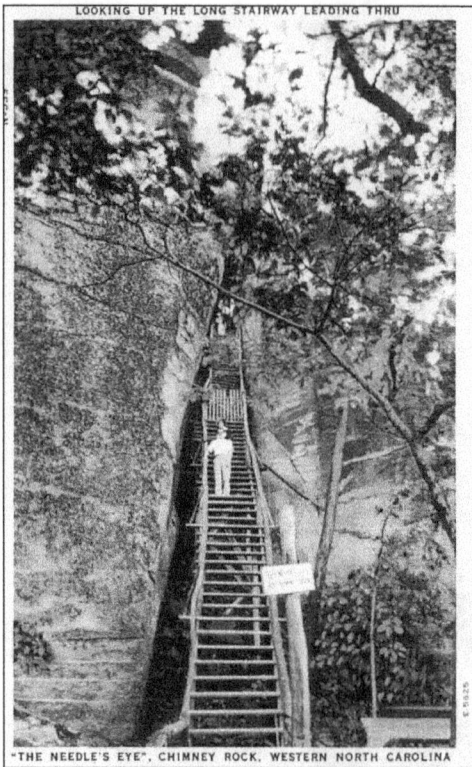

LOOKING UP THE LONG STAIRWAY LEADING THRU

"THE NEEDLE'S EYE", CHIMNEY ROCK, WESTERN NORTH CAROLINA

The Needle's Eye at Chimney Rock is a narrow passage developed within a vertical joint in the granite between the Rock Pile and Pulpit Rock. The top portion of the joint is a mass of boulders and blocks, some of which have fallen into the crack and created the "eye." Guilford Nanney, the man who began the creation of the trail system in the park, constructed the 185 stairs. (Asheville Postcard Company, Asheville, North Carolina.)

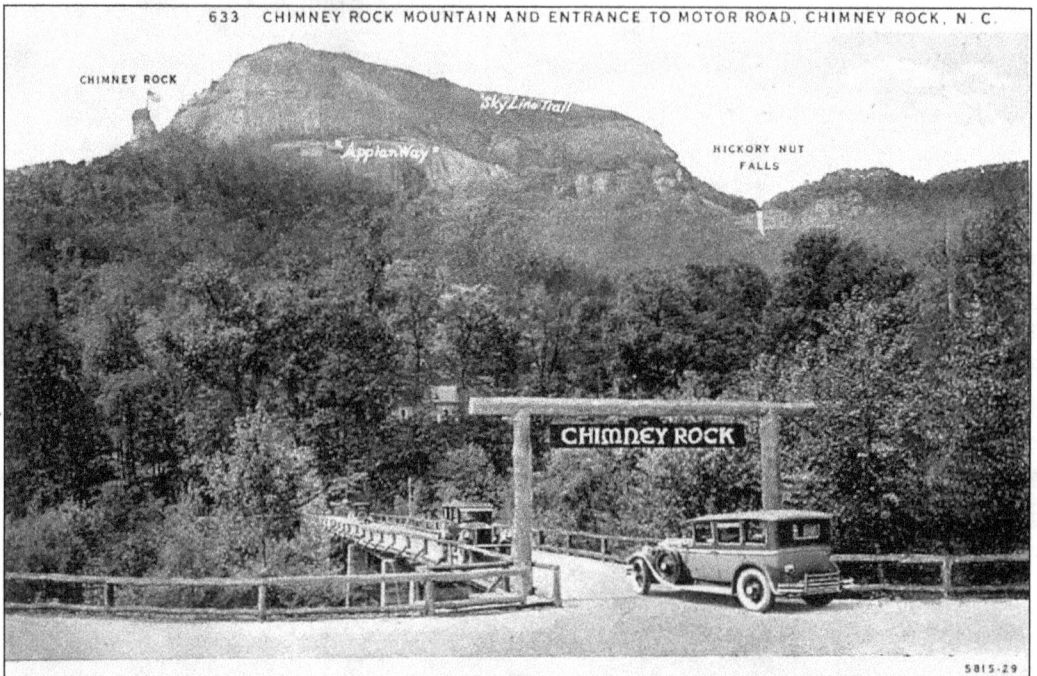

633   CHIMNEY ROCK MOUNTAIN AND ENTRANCE TO MOTOR ROAD, CHIMNEY ROCK, N. C.

This early view of the Chimney Rock Entrance shows a simple wooden sign suspended from a log crosspiece. The natural features in the background are labeled. (Asheville Postcard Company, Asheville, North Carolina.)

This early postcard shows the approach road to Chimney Rock. The road was not hard-surfaced, but there appears to be some added stone to make access to the monolith easier. (Asheville Postcard Company, Asheville, North Carolina.)

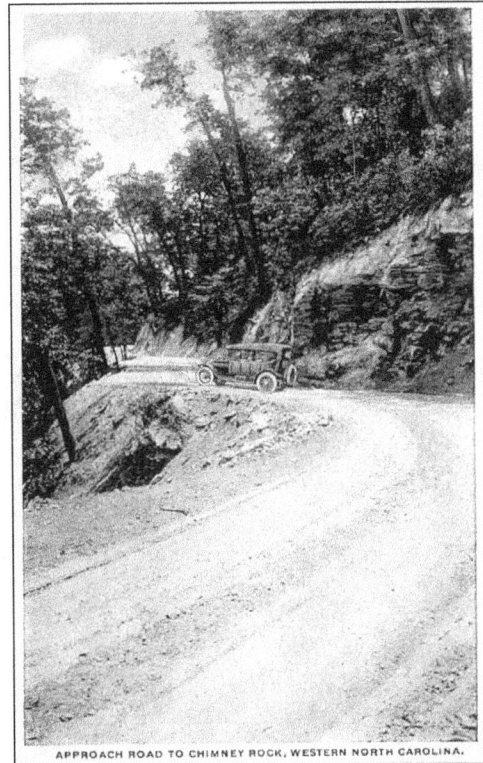

APPROACH ROAD TO CHIMNEY ROCK, WESTERN NORTH CAROLINA.

Originally, visitors to Chimney Rock drove about three miles up the mountain before reaching a tollbooth, where they paid to continue their visit to Chimney Rock and its surrounding trails and vistas. The house located on the right side of the card is still in existence and is used privately by the owners of Chimney Rock Park. (Asheville Postcard Company, Asheville, North Carolina.)

The massive walls, gardens, flower-topped pylons, and fountains later formed the gateway to Chimney Rock and date from 1926. Douglas Ellington, an Asheville architect, designed the gateway and specified the use of rocks that had moss and lichens for these constructions. (Asheville Postcard Company, Asheville, North Carolina.)

This early view of Main Street in Chimney Rock shows a few gift and souvenir stores. The rock python and fountain constructed in 1926 are visible in the lower right hand corner of the card. (Asheville Postcard Company, Asheville, North Carolina.)

16

Contrast the earlier entrance to Chimney Rock on the previous page with the more recent view above. Today's park, located 25 miles southeast of Asheville, has spectacular 75-mile views, numerous hiking trails, a 404-foot waterfall, a Nature Center, picnicking, and more. (Asheville Postcard Company, Asheville, North Carolina.)

613 THE DEVIL'S HEAD, SHOWING ROCKY BROAD RIVER.

© by Pelton.

CHIMNEY ROCK SECTION, WESTERN NORTH CAROLINA   80528

The Devil's Head, carved by nature, overlooks Chimney Rock and the Blue Ridge Mountains in majesty. The sender wrote on the back of the postcard in 1936, "A few feet to the bottom of that baby." (Asheville Postcard Company, Asheville, North Carolina.)

The Mountain View Inn was another place for visitors to stay and enjoy the mountain air and the relaxation of a quiet surrounding. The Mountain View burned in the late 1950s. (Information courtesy of Pete O'Leary, Bubba's, Chimney Rock, North Carolina. Asheville Postcard Company, Asheville, North Carolina.)

N-786   U. S. HIGHWAY NO. 74 BY MOONLIGHT BETWEEN CHIMNEY ROCK & BAT CAVE, N. C.

This postcard shows the paved Highway 20 (now #74) after its completion in July 1927. The last link of the line from Tennessee to Wilmington was from Rutherfordton to Lake Lure. The State Highway Commission borrowed $700,000 from Rutherford County to help finance the road. On July 30, a mammoth celebration brought 20,000 people to Lake Lure. This card shows a portion of the old, two-lane, concrete road between Chimney Rock and Bat Cave. (Asheville Postcard Company, Asheville, North Carolina.)

Around 1920 the Cliff Dweller's Inn had a row of 10 cottages along a ledge at the south of the parking lot. The back wall of the lobby was the five-mile–thick mountain. (Asheville Postcard Company, Asheville, North Carolina.)

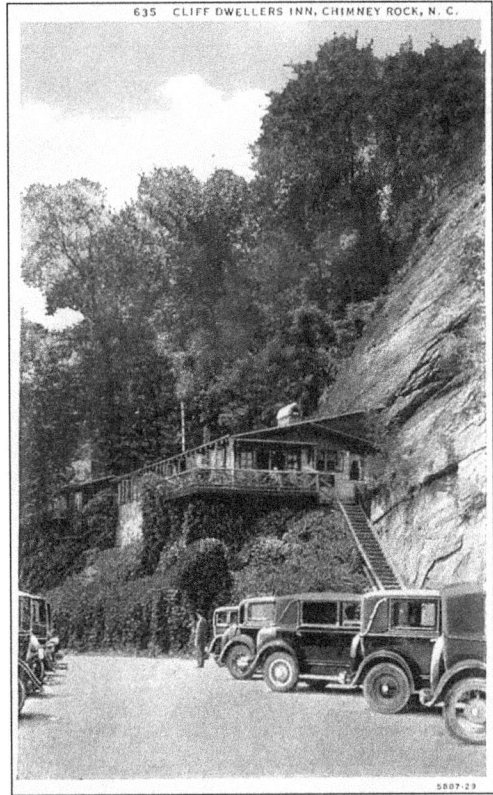

635 CLIFF DWELLERS INN, CHIMNEY ROCK, N. C.

636   DINING ROOM AND LOBBY, CLIFF DWELLERS INN, CHIMNEY ROCK, N. C.

The dining room and lobby of the Cliff Dweller's Inn appear quite formal in this early postcard. The back wall of the dining room and lobby is the rock of the mountain behind it. (Asheville Postcard Company, Asheville, North Carolina.)

19

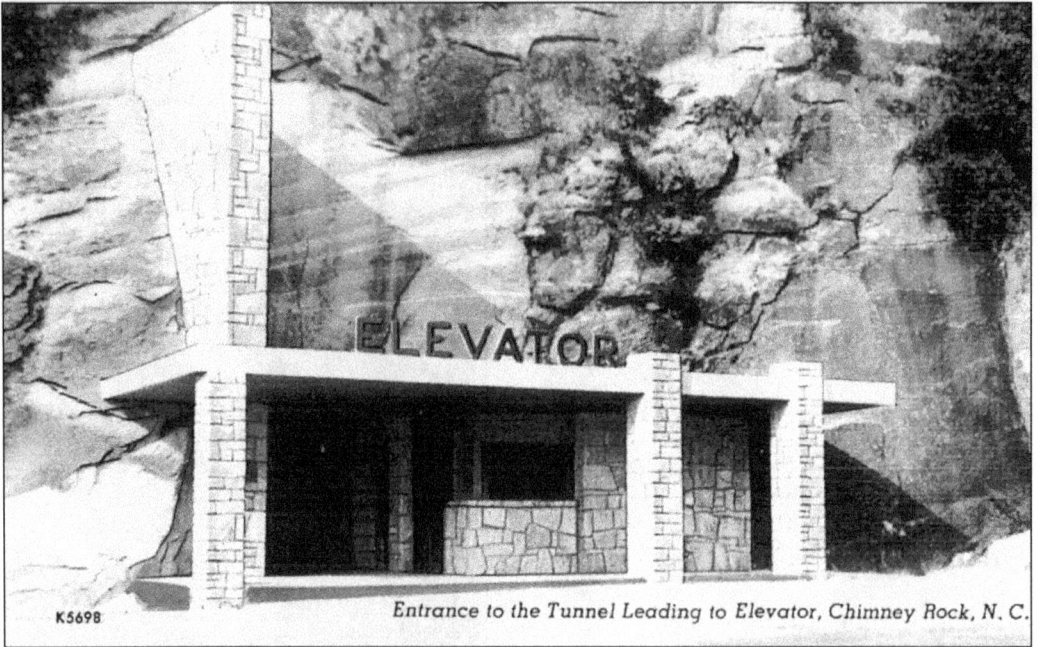

Entrance to the Tunnel Leading to Elevator, Chimney Rock, N. C.

K5698

In 1948-1949 the owners of Chimney Rock installed a modern elevator 198 feet inside the cliff. It took nine months and eight tons of dynamite to open the passage. The elevator carried visitors the 258 feet to the Sky Lounge in only 32 seconds. (Asheville Postcard Company, Asheville, North Carolina.)

234—Tunnel to the Elevator, Chimney Rock, N. C.

OC-H182

To reach the elevator, visitors walk down a 196-foot tunnel that leads to the elevator. The elevator rises 26 floors to the Sky Lounge at Chimney Rock Park. (Curteich-Chicago "C.T. Art-Colortone." Courtesy of Harry N. Martin, P.O. Box 324, Asheville, North Carolina.)

338:-ALONG THE APPIAN WAY, CHIMNEY ROCK SECTION, WESTERN NORTH CAROLINA.

Few panoramas equal the one of the Appian Way from "Inspiration Point." This particular view looks eastward. A unique view of the sublime and the picturesque was evident from this vantage point only a 15-minute walk from Chimney Rock on the trail that Morse and his brothers developed. The area pictured was the future site of Lake Lure. Notice this view was before the construction of Lake Lure, the dam for which closed on September 20, 1926. (Asheville Postcard Company, Asheville, North Carolina.)

723   LAKE LURE FROM APPIAN WAY, WESTERN NORTH CAROLINA

This later panorama of the Appian Way from "Inspiration Point" shows Lake Lure after it was filled in the late 1920s. The view is only a short walk from Chimney Rock. (Asheville Postcard Company, Asheville, North Carolina.)

21

The first Baptist Church in Chimney Rock was the Chimney Rock Baptist Church, formed about 1870. The congregation met in a schoolhouse. When the church disbanded, another church, the Whiteside Valley Church, started in 1892. When the projected Lake Lure Dam seemed likely to take the church, it moved to this location and changed its name to Chimney Rock Baptist Church in 1926. Dr. Lucius Morse has rested in the cemetery adjoining the church since his death on July 15, 1946. Lucius B. Morse III (great nephew of Dr. Morse) and his son Todd Baker Morse (great-great nephew) still own and manage the Chimney Rock Company. (Asheville Postcard Company, Asheville, North Carolina.)

The flood of July 1916 is the greatest storm and flood known to western North Carolina. The historian Samuel Ashe noted that the flood affected Carolinians from Wilkes to Rutherford. He noted that the floods swept away homes, crops, and the very soil of the area. On page 1,251 of his two-volume history, he notes that it was the most disastrous event in the history of that region and that the losses were beyond computation. (Courtesy of W. H. McArthur.)

The Chimney Rock Mountains Corporation was the largest corporation in the state of North Carolina at the time of its charter. Its capitalization was $4,000,00. In March 1925 the corporation let a contract for building a dam across the Rocky Broad River. This photograph shows the dam beginning to impound the water of the Rocky Broad River into a lake. The dam closed on September 20, 1926. (Courtesy of W. H. McArthur.)

Construction work on the Lake Lure Inn began in February 1926. An all-day celebration on June 15 commemorated the laying of the cornerstone. The Fort Bragg Military Band and Gen. A.J. Bowley as speaker gave dignity to the occasion. The Lake Lure Inn was a $400,000 construction. This view shows that Lake Lure is still filling at the time that Will McArthur made the photograph. (Courtesy of W. H. McArthur.)

The magnificent Lake Lure Inn has had many uses. The United States Army leased the inn in the 1940s as a rest center for air corpsmen returning from duty. The inn provided a setting for the 1987 movie *Dirty Dancing* with Patrick Swayze and Jennifer Gray. Such notables as Emily Post, Franklin D. Roosevelt, and F. Scott Fitzgerald used it for rest and relaxation. (Curteich-Chicago Postcard Company.)

On a motor trip on September 10, 1936, from Asheville to the Green Pastures Rally in Charlotte, President Franklin Delano Roosevelt and his party lunched at the Lake Lure Inn. Outside the inn, President Roosevelt waved his hat at the crowd of people, each hoping to catch a glimpse of the President of the United States. The Carolina mountains are clearly visible in the background. (Courtesy of the Lake Lure Inn, Lake Lure, North Carolina.)

This view from about 1938 shows the completed million-dollar dam at Lake Lure. (Asheville Postcard Company, Asheville, North Carolina.)

LAKE LURE, LOOKING TOWARD RUMBLING BALD MOUNTAIN, LAKE LURE, N. C. "IN THE LAND OF THE SKY." B-46

"Rumbling Bald" rises above Lake Lure. It received its name from the echoing sounds coming from within; the *Philadelphia Inquirer* ran an article on the mystery on March 18, 1874. Scientists later found that boulders falling among the caves and tunnels within had created the rumbles. A second mystery is why it will not support the growth of trees. The question has never been answered. Altitude is not the answer because higher tops—even 5,000 feet higher—support tree growth. The mountain without visible forests continues to stand in the midst of hardwood and spruce. (Asheville Postcard Company, Asheville, North Carolina.)

STATE HIGHWAY NO. 20 AROUND LAKE LURE.

This postcard shows the State Highway #20 (now Highway #64/74A) around Lake Lure. The road construction, particularly the surfacing, is not complete. It was July 1927 before this last link (from Rutherfordton to Lake Lure) of the line from Tennessee to Wilmington was completed. (Asheville Postcard Company, Asheville, North Carolina.)

BRIDGE SPANNING ROCKY BROAD RIVER ON STATE ROUTE NO. 20.

BETWEEN LAKE LURE AND CHIMNEY ROCK.

This bridge spans the Rocky Broad River on State Route Number 20 between Lake Lure and Chimney Rock. (Asheville Postcard Company, Asheville, North Carolina.)

This autumn scene from the 1960s shows the Lake Lure Administration Building with Chimney Rock Mountain in the background. (Asheville Postcard Company, Asheville, North Carolina.)

This service station in Lake Lure has an unusual architectural style for most stations in North Carolina. The style is suggestive of Italy and blends in well with the style of the Lake Lure Administration Building and the Lake Lure Inn. (Photo by James M. Walker.)

This postcard dated January 14, 1936 shows the Log Shop at Lake Lure, North Carolina. Located on Lake Lure, this popular restaurant and gift center has long been a favorite of tourists to the area. Even after the turn of the century, the building continued to be in use. While filming the 1958 cult classic movie *Thunder Road*, which depicted moonshine running in the mountains, actor Robert Mitchum often ate at the Log Shop. Betty Bumgardner Conner, who worked as a waitress there, served him. (Information Courtesy of Joann Bumgardner Bridges. Asheville Postcard Company, Asheville, North Carolina.)

CHIMNEY ROCK CAMP FOR BOYS.

The Chimney Rock Camp for Boys was one of the settings used in *Dirty Dancing*, the 1987 movie with Patrick Swayze and Jennifer Gray. The area around Lake Lure, Chimney Rock, and Rumbling Bald Mountain has been the setting for numerous movies, including *The Last of the Mohicans* (1992) with Daniel Day Lewis, Russell Means, and Madeline Stowe. Interestingly, the Italian architecture has enabled movie companies to use North Carolina as a setting for movies set in Italy. (Asheville Postcard Company, Asheville, North Carolina.)

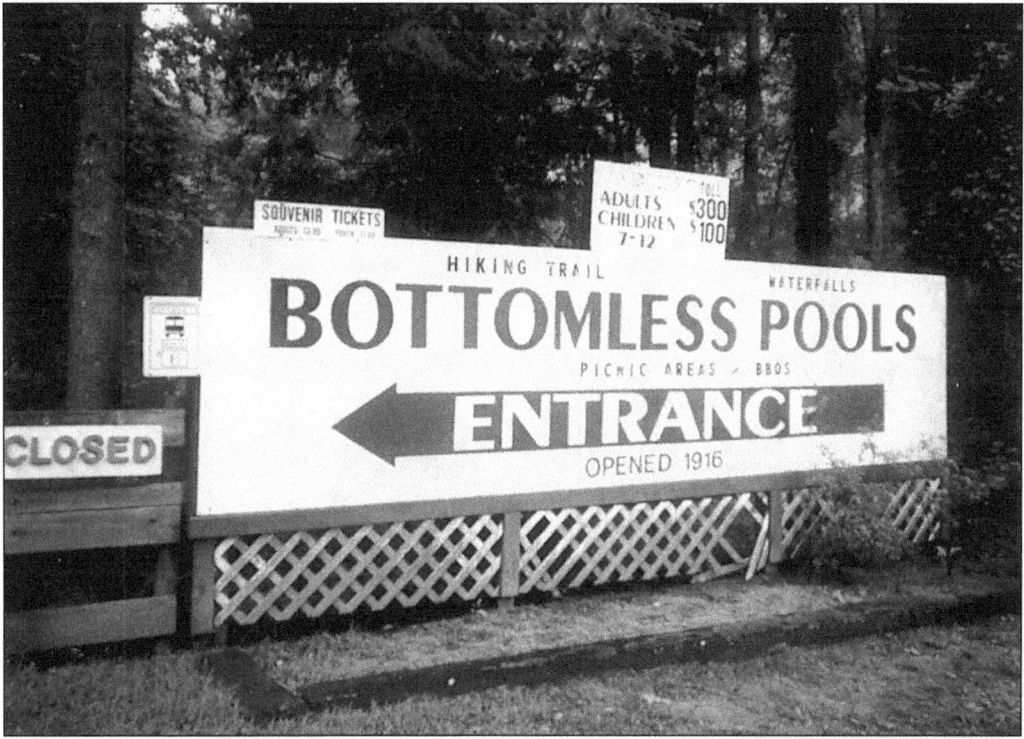

The Bottomless Pools are a natural feature several hundred feet from U.S. Highway #64/74. The natural attraction opened to the public in 1916. The Bottomless Pools are normally opened daily to visitors. (Photo by James M. Walker.)

To reach the Bottomless Pools today, visitors must cross the Pool Creek Covered Bridge. The Bottomless Pools are about 300 yards from Highway 74 in Lake Lure. (Photo by James M. Walker.)

Believe It Or Not - By Robert Ripley

GUSTAVE P. CLUSERET

WAS CAPT. IN THE FRENCH ARMY MAJOR IN THE MEXICAN ARMY LT COLONEL IN THE IRISH ARMY COLONEL IN THE ITALIAN ARMY AND BRIGADIER GENERAL IN THE UNION ARMY DURING CIVIL WAR

SHORTHORN COW GAVE BIRTH TO TRIPLES TWICE IN 11 MONTHS ISLE OF MAN

BOTTOMLESS POOLS RIPLEY JUNE 29, 1939

IN THE HEART OF THE BLUE RIDGE MOUNTAINS THEIR DEPTH HAS NEVER BEEN FATHOMED!

THE BOTTOMLESS POOLS —

AT LAKE LURE, N. C., DEEP IN THE BLUE RIDGE MOUNTAINS, ARE THREE BOTTOMLESS POOLS. THAT SKETCHED IS KNOWN AS THE LOWER POOL AND IS CONSIDERED THE MOST REMARKABLE. IT IS 15 FEET IN DIAMETER, HAS PERPENDICULAR SIDES AND IS WORN PERFECTLY ROUND. NO ONE IS KNOWN TO HAVE FOUND THE BOTTOM!

On June 29, 1939, Ripley's *Believe It Or Not* stated that the depths of these three pools had never been fathomed. (Photo by James M. Walker.)

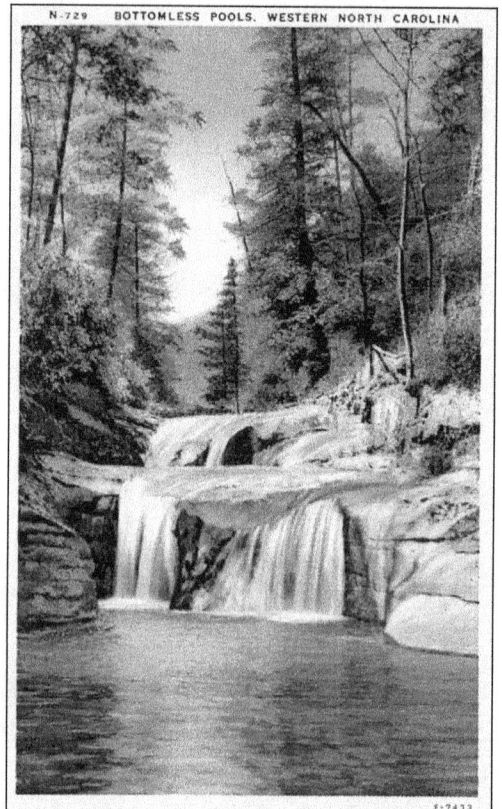

The Bottomless Pools are at least 100,000 and possibly even 500,000 years old. Their formation is the result of soft rock being washed out by the flow of the water and hard rock remaining. This view shows the waterfalls feeding into the Bottomless Pools. (Asheville Postcard Company, Asheville, North Carolina.)

After studying medicine in Germany, Dr. James Murray Washburn visited his son who worked for S.E. Elmore in Rutherford County. The mountains around Lake Lure reminded Dr. Washburn of Germany. When he saw the view from a certain site (now 532 Washburn Road), he immediately bought the land that weekend—without even consulting his wife. His brother-in-law helped design the chalet as a family retreat. Dr. Washburn and his wife opened the Chalet Club as an inn; their son Dick and his wife Dorothy, and later their grandson Bob and his wife Ann, assumed the operation and improvement of the Chalet Club and its additional cottages. This inn is reminiscent of a scene from the Swiss Alps. (Photo by James M. Walker.)

This postcard (probably from the 1930s) shows the Club Room of the Chalet Club.

In 1999 Pine Gables was added to the National Register of Historic Places. Located at 328 Boys Camp Road in Lake Lure, Pine Gables (known originally as the Harris Inn, later known as the Logan House, and still later as the Red Coach Inn) was a stagecoach inn in the late 1700s and is the oldest structure that was used as an inn in Rutherford County. The first post office at Chimney Rock was established at the inn on December 19, 1843. During the Great Depression, the inn and surrounding property were used as a CCC camp. Major renovations were performed on the house in 1834, 1877, and 1936; its architectural style is Queen Anne. Frances Hodgson Burnett wrote *Esmeralda* here. (Photo by James M. Walker.)

The Davenport-Edgerton House on Bills Creek Road in Uree was built in three stages. John Davenport had the one-story rear wall constructed in 1800, and Benjamin F. Edgerton added the two-story front section after the Civil War. The two-story porch appears to be the work of Guilford Nanny who helped with the wooden constructions at Chimney Rock Park. (Photo by James M. Walker.)

Two

GREEN HILL, UNION, AND SULPHUR SPRINGS, TOWNSHIPS

Green Hill, Union, and Sulphur Springs Townships form the western border of Rutherford County, and Polk County borders the three townships on the west. South Carolina joins Sulphur Springs Township, the most southern of the three townships. The northern and eastern borders of all three townships are other Rutherford County townships. Of the three townships, Green Hill is the most northern—it lies between Maple and Mountain Creeks. This look at the three townships will begin with Green Hill Township, will view Union Township to its south, and will consider lastly the Sulphur Springs Township.

The Green Hill Volunteer Fire Department serves the community well in case of emergency. In addition, the facility at 2711 on Highway 64/74A provides the polling place for Green Hill Township. (Photo by James M. Walker.)

The J.W. Whiteside House is a weather-boarded, two-story house that was originally a log dwelling sometime in the late 1700s. Through the years its owners have enlarged the house. The south front has two shed additions. In 1884, Zachary Taylor Whiteside moved into the house and added an ell with two-tiered porches on the north side. (Photo by James M. Walker.)

In more recent years the Whiteside Farm on Highway #64/74A has become known as "Pumpkin Center" because of its ample yearly harvest of the vine crop.

The Green Hill School, originally a community school, was an important part of the community. According to the plaque on the wall, the board of education erected Green Hill School in 1921. Consolidation has, however, provided other facilities for the students of the area. Elementary students began attending the newly erected Pinnacle School in 2000. (Photo by James M. Walker.)

The Green Hill Community Center on Highway 64/74A is an important structure to the residents of the Green Hill community. Without a community school, this center provides residents of Green Hill with a facility for events. (Photo by James M. Walker.)

In 1972, the National Register of Historical Places listed the Fox Haven Plantation at the Polk-Rutherford County line and off State Road 1157. Located in the Green Hill Township, this historical site was built between 1800 and 1824. (Photo by James M. Walker.)

The William G. Miller House was built in the 1880s. The steep roof has multiple gables and its design reflects the influence and work of the Italian Monfredo brothers and A.J. Downing. Miller's wife ran a post office in a log building near the house. (Photo by James M. Walker.)

Grays Chapel Methodist Church is probably a rebuilding of a meetinghouse built in 1852. The church's date is anywhere from the mid-19th to early 20th century. A log structure was erected in 1825 for David Gray, the church leader at the time. In 1861, Gray deeded to the congregation the land on which the building stands. The frame church is believed to be one of the oldest churches in the county.(Photo by James M. Walker.)

Important in the Sulphur Springs Township is the Shiloh community, located near the headwaters of Jarretts Creek. The Shiloh Baptist Church held its first meeting in 1833 and had, as its first building, a log structure. A frame building replaced the log church. The third building, built in 1910, had stained glass windows. In 1940 the building burned. The fourth church is a brick structure with full basement. Numerous improvements continue to be made. William Ruppe and Mack Sane, both of whom were killed during World War II, were members of Shiloh Baptist Church. (Photo by James M. Walker.)

Cleghorn reached completion in the 1830s. Originally built for Thomas McEntire, the stuccoed brick plantation house is located at the union of the Broad River and Cleghorn Creek. The bricks for the hip-roofed structure came from Cleghorn Creek. The father of Dr. Ben Washburn (associated with Rutherford Hospital, the *Progressive Farmer,* and health departments at home and abroad) purchased the structure in 1889. Ben Washburn later sold the property to Dr. G.O. Moss. (Photo by James M. Walker.)

Nat Hamrick Sr. purchased Cleghorn and the surrounding property from Dr. G.O. Moss and developed it into a country club. There is a dining room, a golf course, tennis courts, a pool, and a residential section in the Cleghorn vicinity. A frequent golfer at Cleghorn, the Municipal Golf Course in Forest City, and Meadowbrook Golf Course in Caroleen was Thomas C. Thompson Jr. (October 14, 1933–August 31, 1996). Thompson studied with club professional Don Morrow at the Municipal Golf Course and played for more than 30 years. (Courtesy of Mary Fredrick Thompson.)

A resident of the Harris community, Milton Robinson Jr. graduated in 1958 from Carver High School. He played on the Carver football team in 1958 when they won the District III Championship. Milton also played basketball that year. He later attended North Carolina College in Durham, North Carolina. (Courtesy of Milton Robinson Jr.)

Pictured is Victoria Simmons, the great-grandmother of Milton Robinson Jr. Mrs. Simmons was a former slave born in the 1800s. She lived to see freedom before her death in 1932. (Courtesy of Milton Robinson Jr.)

Milton Robinson Jr.'s grandmother was Clementine Mosely Withrow and his mother was Lois Robinson (December 16, 1916–December 28, 1993), a resident of the Harris community. Like most Rutherford County men in times of war and the draft, he willingly entered the service. He married on July 10, 1960, at the McClintock Presbyterian Church in Charlotte, North Carolina. His wife Ruth followed him from 1960 through 1969 on many of his six major moves in the army and as an employee of Southern Bell in Atlanta. Mr. and Mrs. Robinson returned to the Harris community after his retirement and her retirement from the public schools. (Courtesy of Mr. and Mrs. Milton Robinson Jr.)

The Harris Speedway, located in Harris, North Carolina, has an oval, three-eighths-of-a-mile dirt track. It has been a popular recreational area for Rutherford County residents. (Photo by James M. Walker.)

Three

MORGAN, GILKEY, AND CAMP CREEK TOWNSHIPS

Morgan Township and Camp Creek Township are two of the five most northern townships in Rutherford County. McDowell County borders both of the townships to the north. Gilkey Township and Green Hill Township form a southern border for the two. To the west of Gilkey and Camp Creek lies Logan's Store Township. Important areas within the Morgan Township include Shingle Hollow, Whitehouse, and Montford Cove.

The Shingle Hollow community is south of Toms Mountain in Morgan Township. The Shingle Hollow Fire Department serves the area. In the same building as the fire department at 2621 Cove Road is the Shingle Hollow Community Center, which can double as a polling place. (Photo by James M. Walker.)

One of the most modern sanctuaries in design in Morgan Township is the Shingle Hollow Congregational Holiness Church, located at 2466 Cove Road. The family center for the congregation is visible to the left of the picture. (Photo by James M. Walker.)

The Montford Cove Missionary Baptist Church is in the Whitehouse community of Morgan Township. Whitehouse community lies between Cove and Otter Creeks. In the 18th century, a stockade for the protection of settlers was in the vicinity of Montford Cove Church. Turner Robbins and Huland Harris, two residents of the Montford Cove community, were killed during World War II. (Photo by James M. Walker.)

Antioch Baptist Church on Bills Creek Road near Whitehouse is a simple chapel that has remained surprisingly unchanged since its construction, which was probably during the 1800s. A transom is visible above the double front doors, which provide entrance into the sanctuary. The windows are plain, not stained glass. (Photo by James M. Walker.)

The Gilkey Township received its name from the Gilkey community within its borders. Until it was renamed for a local family, the community was known as Milwood. The Morgan and Camp Creek Townships border Gilkey Township to the north. Its border on the east is Logan's Store Township; Green Hill and Rutherfordton Townships lie to its south. Gilkey School is the primary landmark in Gilkey community. (Photo by James M. Walker.)

Camp Creek Township is bordered on the west by Morgan Township, on the south by Gilkey Township, and on the east/southeast by Logan's Store Township. Union Mills and Thermal City are two of the communities within Camp Creek Township. A thermal belt is an area that has a more even—and often milder—temperature than comparable regions with similar altitude and latitude. Thermal City, on the second Broad River in Camp Creek Township, received its name from its unusual—and usually milder—weather patterns. Known originally as Pescud, its post office opened in 1888. Pescud became Thermal City in 1891. The Thermal City Methodist Church dates from 1924. (Photo by James M. Walker.)

One of the earliest gold mines in Rutherford County was at the Rutherford and McDowell County line in the Camp Creek Township (1830). In 1880, Amos Nanney bought the land, which is still in the Nanney family. Little mining, was done, however, during the 1900s—except during the Great Depression—until the Thermal City Gold and Gem Mine opened to the public in 1992. The attraction attempts to give guests a chance to mine for gold or gems in their natural state. By searching the gravel that two backhoes take from the pit and a truck delivers to the work area, patrons have the opportunity for an authentic mining experience. (Information courtesy of Floyd Nanney, 828-286-3016. Photo by James M. Walker.)

Inside the entrance to the Thermal City Gold and Gem Mine, patrons see a rock crusher from the early 1910s—rare indeed in our nation—and a building suggestive of the gold mining days. (Photo copyrighted by Ingrid V. Coyle, 2001, and used with permission.)

The process that guests use is much like that in mines across the world. Pay gravels are fed into the hopper and are then washed into the trommel. This trommel is one of the few operating in the Eastern United States today. Screens or holes punched in the wash barrel separate the coarser rock from the smaller particles, which hopefully contain pay dirt. (Photos furnished by and used with permission of Thermal City Gold Mine, 828-286-3016.)

A historic landmark in the Thermal City community is the "Pete Weaver House." Built by A.F. Weaver Sr. more than 100 years ago, the two-story structure with the large front porch reminds one of an earlier time when families had time to visit and talk. When the Henderson Green Weaver home at the same location burned, A.F. Weaver Sr. built this house in the exact same place. (Photo by James M. Walker.)

Union Mills—formerly Crab Apple Gap—took its new name from the sawmills that fused with the construction of the Southern Railway (1890) and the Carolina, Clinchfield, and Ohio Railroad (CC&O) in the early 1900s. The establishment of Union Mills (Camp Creek Township) was in 1892 and its incorporation was in 1907 before the repeal of its charter in 1924. The Union Mills Post Office (28167) is important to the people in Camp Creek Township. This scene shows the bulletin board on which residents can post announcements, notices, and messages for others. (Courtesy of Christine Ammons and the Post Mark Collectors Club.)

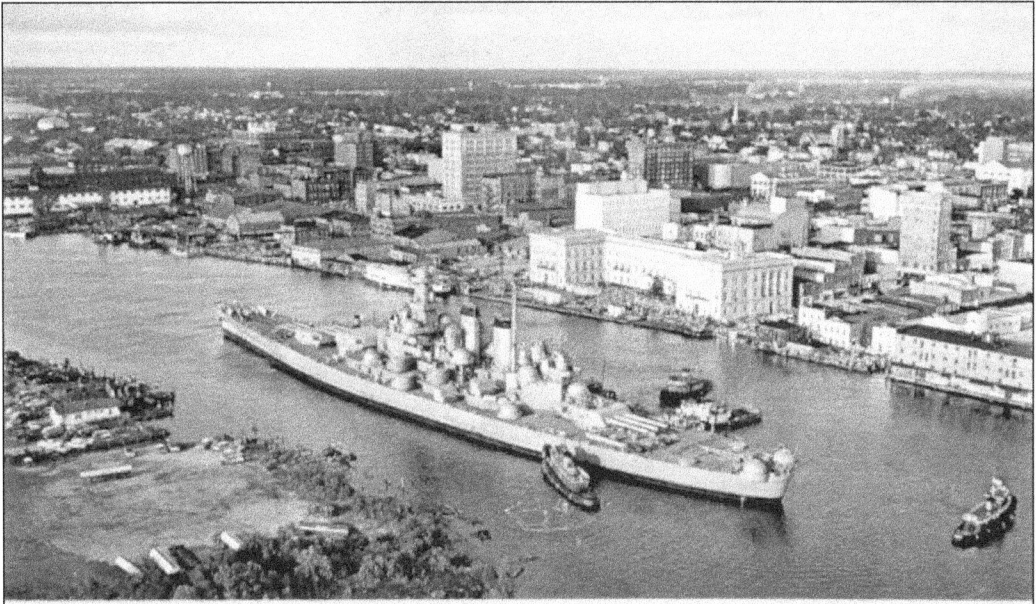

U.S.S. North Carolina "Comes Home" October 2, 1961

On October 2, 1961, the USS *North Carolina* arrived in her permanent berth: across the river from downtown Wilmington. The North Carolina Roll of Honor on the USS *North Carolina* lists those from North Carolina who were killed in World War II and includes those from Rutherford County. Commissioned on April 9, 1941, the battleship was at the time the greatest sea weapon the United States had ever built. She sailed in and out of New York Harbor so many times that she obtained the nickname "Show Boat." She participated in 12 Asiatic-Pacific campaigns during World War II. (Courtesy of USS *North Carolina* Battleship Memorial.)

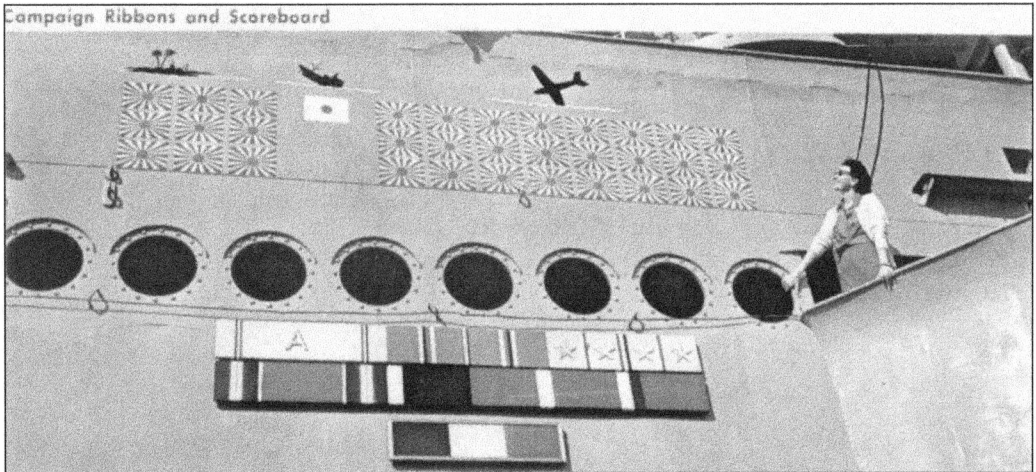

Campaign Ribbons and Scoreboard

The USS *North Carolina* had one of the most extensive battle records in the U.S. Navy's history. She participated in every major offensive engagement in the Pacific in World War II, from Guadalcanal to Tokyo Bay. The USS *North Carolina* earned 12 battle stars. The people of North Carolina and their friends raised over $300,000 to establish the ship as a memorial to those in the military services in World War II. (Courtesy of USS *North Carolina* Battleship Memorial.)

The formation of the Camp Creek Baptist Church was in 1822. The first building was of logs and was located approximately where the center of the current cemetery is. Later, the church members paid for a frame structure. In 1948 the church members paid to turn the church more than 100 degrees northeast to provide more room for the educational facilities. (Photo by James M. Walker.)

African-American parishioners formed the Mount Pleasant C.M.E. Church in Union Mills, North Carolina, in the early 1900s. Unusual features of the church, which is still in use, include the two uneven towers in the front and the round steps. (Photo by James M. Walker.)

James Harvey Forney completed his home in 1859. The two-story entrance porch with a peaked roof and latticework adorn the feature. Scalloped bargeboards outline both the eaves and the porch. Otherwise the house is a standard, two-story, frame house. It is uncertain if the decorative features were a part of the original structure or if Forney added them to his home, located on State Road 1504 in Union Mills. (Photo by James M. Walker.)

Round Hill Baptist Church is located at 6585 Hudlow Road in Union Mills near the site of the original 1840 church. The brick structure looks toward the cemetery and the markers commemorating Round Hill Academy. (Photo by James M. Walker.)

The first reference to Round Hill Academy in the Green River Baptist Association records was in 1899. The building that was almost completed at that time was to be a two-story structure, with a 15-feet-by-32-feet front vestibule, and with six rooms. The maximum capacity of the structure was 300 students. The objective of the academy was to prepare both boys and girls for Wake Forest, Baptist Female University (later Meredith College), or any college in which the students might be interested. Round Hill Academy was in the Union Mills area. (*Round Hill Academy: 1899–1926.* Published by Liberty Press, Rutherfordton, North Carolina.)

The closing of Round Hill Academy at Union Mills (also known as Alexander Schools, Inc.) was on December 23, 1926. Across the road from Round Hill Baptist Church, a round, granite stone commemorates Round Hill Academy. (Photo by James M. Walker.)

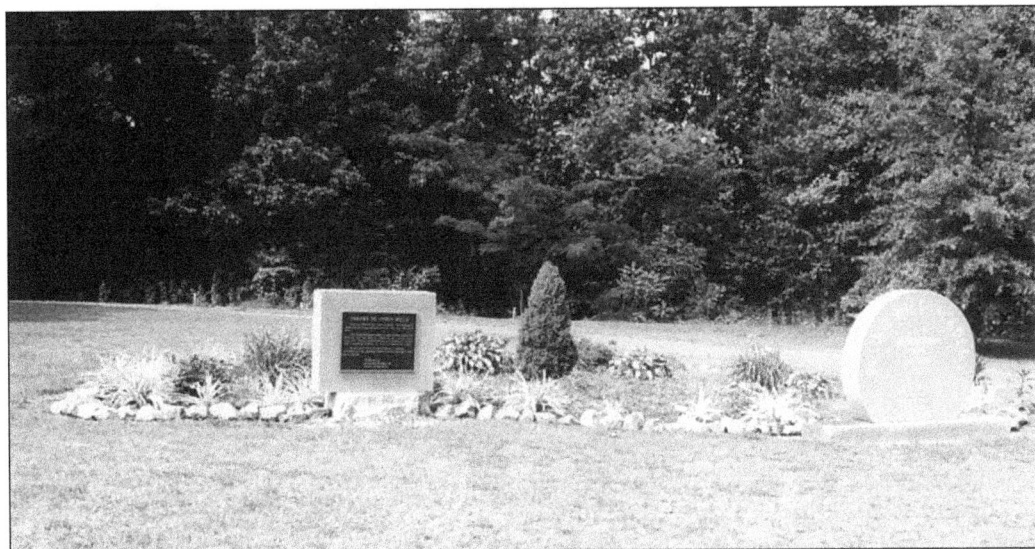

At the side of the round, granite stone, a dedication marker reads, "Thanks to Union Mills. God has blessed this spot on Earth. He blessed us with a faculty so grand and teachers who were second to none. The thing that impressed us most about Alexander School, Inc., was that no visitor to our campus could ever have distinguished between a community student and a boarding student; we were all treated the same. Thanks be to God for allowing us to attend and thanks to the gracious community for making us feel so at HOME. Dedicated by Alexander School, Inc., Alumni Association." (Photo by James M. Walker.)

Farming was important to the area. Even those with salaried positions often maintained gardens to benefit their family. Although this photograph is from the 1930s, the use of the mule for farming continued for more than half a century in the Rutherford County area and elsewhere in the South. (Courtesy of Imogene Foshee Dillon.)

The class of 1912 from Round Hill Academy (later known as Alexander Schools, Inc.) consisted of, from left to right, (front row) Mettie Morgan, Willie Mae Hampton, Zeruh Guffey, and Mamie Simpson; (back row) Bob Gray, N. Lloyd Hampton, and Bert A. Brown. (*Round Hill Academy: 1899–1926*. Published by Liberty Press, Rutherfordton, North Carolina.)

Four

RUTHERFORDTON
TOWNSHIP

Rutherfordton Township has six other townships as its borders. To the north are Gilkey and Logan's Store Townships. To the east are Logan's Store and Cool Springs Townships. Green Hill and Union Townships lie to the west. Sulphur Springs Township forms its southern boundary. Three of the most important towns in Rutherfordton Township are Ruth, Rutherfordton, and Spindale.

One of the main towns within Rutherfordton Township is that of Rutherfordton, which is the county seat of Rutherford County. The National Register of Historical Places added the Main Street Historic District of Rutherfordton with its Colonial Revival, Classical Revival, and Early Commercial Styles to its listings in 1995. This postcard scene from a much earlier time reflects some of this important architecture. (Asheville Postcard Company, Asheville, North Carolina.)

Birdseye View of Rutherfordton, N. C.

This earlier "Birdseye View" of Rutherfordton, North Carolina, shows the dirt road leading to the county seat. Mailed in 1910 from Pastor T.C. Holland of Mooresboro, this card was sent to a couple in his congregation. The postcard was made in Germany for Paul E. Trouche.

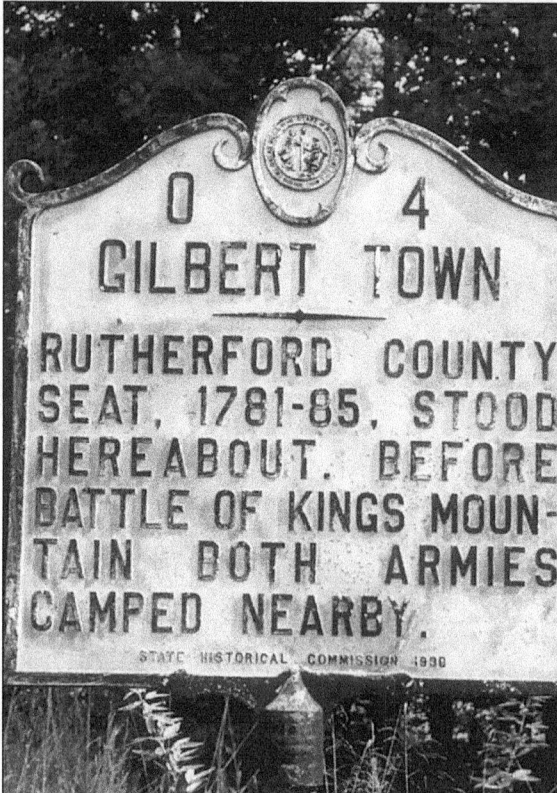

0   4
GILBERT TOWN

RUTHERFORD COUNTY SEAT, 1781-85, STOOD HEREABOUT. BEFORE BATTLE OF KINGS MOUNTAIN BOTH ARMIES CAMPED NEARBY.

STATE HISTORICAL COMMISSION 1936

The county seat of Rutherford County from 1781 to 1785 was originally Gilbert Town. This historical marker from the State Historical Commission of 1936 identifies the site of Gilbert Town (near present-day Rutherfordton) and indicates that, before the Battle of Kings Mountain, both armies camped nearby. (Photo by James M. Walker.)

This photograph shows the second Rutherford County Courthouse in Rutherfordton. The structure, completed in 1836, burned on December 24, 1907. The use of the photograph is from *The History of Old Tryon and Rutherford Counties.* (Courtesy of Tom Smith of Reprint Company, Spartanburg, South Carolina.)

The third Rutherford County Courthouse, completed in 1908, was in use until 1925. The postmark on this postcard is 1909. The postcard was made in Germany for Paul E. Trouche.

Rutherford County's New Court House, Rutherfordton, N. Car.

The laying of the cornerstone of the fourth Rutherfordton County Courthouse was on January 13, 1926. The building was complete by October 1926 at a cost of $250,000, and the dedication was on November 3, 1926. The unveiling ceremony for the Confederate monument had taken place on November 12, 1910. The monument of North Carolina granite with a Confederate soldier of Italian marble cost $2,500. The Rutherford County Courthouse was added to the National Register of Historic Places in 1979. (Auburn Postcard Company, Auburn, Indiana.)

For almost a quarter of a century, the Rutherford County Sheriff's Department had as its leader Damon Huskey. Huskey served from 1958 to 1970 and from 1974 to 1986—a total of 24 years. This calendar shows Huskey and his staff in the year 1984. (Courtesy of Damon Huskey and Mrs. Nell Burns.)

An important Rutherford County hotel was the Iso-thermal Hotel in Rutherfordton. It was originally a frame building erected in 1890. The two-story structure had 43 rooms. When it burned, W.S. Guthrie (the owner) built a new establishment on the premises of his wife's childhood home. Dr. Henry Norris from Pennsylvania and Mary Mathilda Mills Norris stayed in Western North Carolina for their honeymoon. Their love for the area brought them back many times. They often stayed at the Iso-Thermal (later Isothermal) Hotel. This hotel was the lodging place also of such notables as John Barrymore and John L. Lewis. (Courtesy of Liberty Press, Rutherfordton, North Carolina.)

In 1920, S.B. Tanner bought the hotel from Guthrie, and in 1924 he built a three-story, brick structure, which he called the Isothermal. The Isothermal was the site of many social events for the county. It is, however, no longer standing. (Asheville Postcard Company, Asheville, North Carolina.)

In 1890, Capt. William T.R. Bell, who had been born in Virginia, established the Rutherford Military Institute in Rutherfordton. Dr. Henry Norris and Dr. M.H. Biggs, young Philadelphia physicians, started the Rutherford Hospital in the summer of 1906 in the building of the old Rutherford Military Institute. (*Rutherford County and Its Hospital* by B.E. Washburn. Spindale, North Carolina: The Spindale Press, 1960.)

Mrs. Henry Norris (Mary Mathilda Mills Norris) and her mother were Episcopalians. They worshiped for a while at Rutherfordton's St. Francis Church, the only Episcopal church in the county at the turn of the century. The building, a replica of a 14th-century English countryside church, was built using locally quarried stone. Construction began in 1898 and local craftsmen and stonemasons made the building more meaningful. This card was postmarked May 15, 1911.

Because they were accustomed to the "high" church rituals, ceremonies, and services of the Episcopal Church of Philadelphia, Mrs. Norris and her mother arranged for the construction on the grounds of Rutherford Hospital of a chapel that would have formal services to meet their needs. Named after the biblical physician, St. Luke's Chapel opened in the fall of 1907. The single-room structure with a simple altar and frosted windowpanes remained unchanged until the addition of a library in 1915. The National Register of Historic Places added the chapel, at the junction of Hospital Drive and Old Twitty Ford Road in Rutherfordton, to its list in 1991. (Photo by James M. Walker.)

The official opening of a newly constructed, brick building called Rutherford Hospital was on March 9, 1911. Notice that there are no paved roads in this early card. This postcard was published by Dr. F.B. Twitty Drug Company, The Rexall Store, in Rutherfordton. The official donation of the hospital to Rutherford County was in 1925. At that time its new name was Rutherford County Hospital.

Many additions through the years have kept the Rutherford County Hospital as one of the best in the nation. The addition of the Norris-Briggs Memorial Wing in 1951 was an impressive addition. (*Rutherford County and Its Hospital* by B.E. Washburn. Spindale, North Carolina: Spindale Press, 1960.)

The National Register of Historic Places added the George W. Logan House (State Road 1555 at U.S. Highway 64) to its registry in 1986. The year of construction of this Georgian house was 1842. The single-dwelling home with outbuildings was the residence of Judge George W. Logan. (Photo by James M. Walker.)

The National Register of Historic Places listed a second Rutherfordton house of worship in its records. Trinity Lutheran Church (also named St. John's Episcopal Church) at 702 North Main Street in Rutherfordton represents the period 1825–1849. Of the Greek-Revival style, the appearance of the structure has remained remarkably similar to an earlier time. (Photo by James M. Walker.)

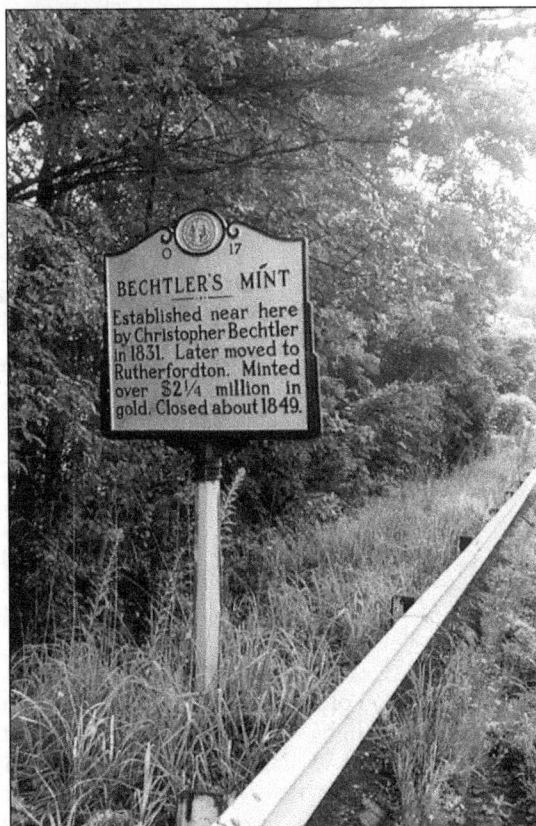

Another Rutherfordton listing in the National Register of Historic Places is the Bechtler's Mint. The roadside marker from the Division of Archives and History indicates that Christopher Bechtler established the mint in 1831 and later moved it to the town of Rutherfordton. Before it closed in 1849, Bechtler's Mint imprinted over $2 1/4 million in gold. (Photo by James M. Walker.)

Main Street in Rutherfordton is the location of the Carrier Houses. Also known as the Carrier-Ward House and the Carrier-McBrayer House, these two homes at 415 and 423 North Main Street in Rutherfordton demonstrate the Queen Anne architectural style. Built by the tinsmith and carpenter Harvey Dewey Carrier in 1835, the Carrier-McBrayer House was his private residence. The Carrier-Ward House was a gift in 1879 to his youngest daughter Margaret on her marriage to Kinchen J. Carpenter. The National Register of Historic Places listed these sites in 1992; both homes are used today as bed and breakfast sites. Pictured above is the Carrier-McBrayer House. (Photo by James M. Walker.)

The construction of Rutherfordton-Spindale Central High School (now called Rutherfordton-Spindale Junior High) was in the 1920s. Located at the junction of Charlotte Road (U.S. Highway 74 Business) and U.S. Highway 74, in the northwest corner in Rutherfordton, this structure with its Classical-Revival architectural style became an addition of the National Register of Historic Places in 1993. (Asheville Postcard Company, Asheville, North Carolina.)

First organized in 1851, the First Baptist Church of Rutherfordton began with 25 members. The church was originally a frame structure across the street from St. Francis's Episcopal Church. In 1880, the church began building the first brick church in the county; the structure served well until 1923 when the locals tore it down in order to build a new, larger building. When fire destroyed it in 1941, the congregation constructed yet another building. (Asheville Postcard Company, Asheville North Carolina.)

Parades were ways to meet neighbors, shop, and enjoy some inexpensive entertainment for the whole family. This Shriner's Parade around the 1920s in Rutherfordton has brought quite a crowd. (Courtesy of the North Carolina Office of Archives and History.)

63

This is an exterior view of Citizens Bank and Trust Company in 1910 in Rutherfordton. (Courtesy of the North Carolina Office of Archives and History.)

This is an interior view of the Rexall Drugstore in Rutherfordton. The photograph dates from 1910. (Courtesy of the North Carolina Office of Archives and History.)

This oxcart in front of Mills Grocery Store in Rutherfordton must have been an unusual sight even in 1907 for a photographer to have snapped the picture. (Courtesy of the North Carolina Office of Archives and History.)

August 21, 1923, marked the incorporation of Spindale. The first board of aldermen included J.Y. Yelton, M.D. Haney, P.H. Grose, J.O. Williams, and G.B. Howard. S.E. Elmore was the mayor. An important landmark is the Spindale House, which K.S. Tanner and family members presented to Spindale. The house was officially open on February 22, 1925. It had formerly been the home of Col. Frank Coxe; the building was to serve for the recreation of the people of Spindale. The building was also to serve as a memorial to Simpson Bobo Tanner, the "pioneer manufacturer of Rutherford County," his wife, and son—all deceased.

UNION CHURCH AT SPINDALE, N. C.   WHERE RELIGIOUS SERVICES ARE HELD BY ALL DENOMINATIONS.

The Union Church of Spindale provided a place where "religious services were held for all denominations." (Southern Postcard Company, Asheville, North Carolina.)

Since 1940, the Mitchell Fabric Company in Spindale has provided the county with a source for material. Many residents remember the grab box with its remnants at discounted prices. More than half a century later the Mitchell Company was still in operation. (Photo by Anita P. Davis.)

After the general assembly established the Department of Community Colleges in 1963, Rutherford County voted 16 to 1 for a $500,000 bond issue to construct a community college. The board of trustees chose the name Isothermal Community College in 1964. The vocational and technical division, which had been operating through Gaston Technical Institute, began operating in 1965 as part of the Isothermal Community College. Until the new buildings were ready for occupancy, the college began working out of temporary locations in Caroleen, Spindale, and Avondale. The photograph above shows the Avondale School, a temporary location for Isothermal Community College. (Courtesy of Isothermal Community College, Spindale, North Carolina.)

The photograph to the right shows the construction of one of the first buildings on campus. President Fred J. Eason inspects the beginning structure. (Courtesy of Isothermal Community College, Spindale, North Carolina.)

The first three buildings opened on the Spindale campus in 1968. This photograph shows two of them. (Courtesy of Isothermal Community College, Spindale, North Carolina.)

The building above is The Foundation, which opened in the 1980s and provides seating for 1,400. A center for learning and the arts, the facility opened in 1999 with a performance by the North Carolina Symphony Orchestra. (Photo by James M. Walker.)

Five

LOGAN'S STORE, GOLDEN VALLEY, AND DUNCAN'S CREEK

Logan's Store, Golden Valley, and Duncan's Creek Townships are located to the northeast of Rutherfordton Township. McDowell and Burke Counties border Logan's Store and Duncan's Creek Townships to the north. Cleveland County borders Golden Valley and Duncan's Creek Townships to the east; other Rutherford County townships form the other borders of Logan's Store and Golden Valley Townships. Important in the development of the townships have been the communities of Westminster, Sunshine, Logan, Golden Valley, and Hollis.

The Logan community received its name from a local storekeeper. The post office for Logan was established before 1882 in Logan's Store but is no longer in business. An important feature of the early community was the gristmill that John Cansalor opened in 1830. The frame mill house by the creek may contain parts of the 1830 structure, which James M. Andrews enlarged and equipped with a cupola in the 1870s. The mill with its stone foundation is the most ancient of the early corn mills in Rutherford County. The Andrews Mill is part of a Rutherford County Historic District listed in the National Register of Historic Places. (Photo by James M. Walker.)

The Andrews House is a two-story frame house and has Colonial-Revival detail and a wraparound porch. Benjamin Andrews erected the building in 1907. The Andrews House is part of a Rutherford County Historic District listed in the National Register of Historic Places. (Photo by James M. Walker.)

BIGGERSTAFF
HANGING TREE

Returning from the battle of Kings Mountain, the victorious "Over Mountain Men" hung nine of the captured Tories from a tree near this spot October 14, 1780.

The community of Sunshine is on Robinson Creek. J.W. Biggerstaff, who had a store there, named the community before 1881. Loyalists to Great Britain were numerous in the Sunshine area and in Rutherford County during the 1700s. Perhaps this was one reason that the Over Mountain Men hung nine captured Tory soldiers from a tree in Biggerstaff's Field on October 14, 1780. (Photo by James M. Walker.)

Brittain Presbyterian Church (1768) is the oldest church in Rutherford County and the oldest church west of the Catawba River. It is located in the Westminster community. It has had three buildings: a log structure, one on the Union Mills Road, and an 1852 structure that was brick veneered in the 1940s, has been modernized several times, and is still in use. (Photo by James M. Walker.)

Making molasses is an art. This postcard depicts the grinding of the cane by mule to extract the sweet juice. The juice will flow from the press into a vat, and after boiling the syrup for just the right time, the worker will obtain sorghum molasses for the use of the family or for sale. (Asheville Postcard Company, Asheville, North Carolina.)

The Westminster community grew up around Fort McGaughey, which dates from 1765 and was in use during the Revolution. Westminster community took its name from Westminster School founded in 1901 by 10 Presbyterian churches in Rutherford, Polk, and Cleveland Counties. The school closed in 1923. This photograph shows Westminster School about 1908. (Courtesy of the North Carolina Office of Archives and History.)

This photograph shows a baseball game on the athletic field at Westminster School about 1913. (Courtesy of the North Carolina Office of Archives and History.)

Rutherford County contributed 5,000 men to World War II; 149 were killed. After World War II, families of those buried on foreign soil had a choice as to whether to bring the body back to the United States or to allow it to remain abroad. The family of Pfc. John A. Morris, 27 years old, elected to bring his body back to the United States and to inter the body in the Mount Vernon Cemetery. (Courtesy of Walda Carpenter.)

The Golden Valley Township is located in the most northeastern corner of Rutherford County. The Golden Valley community is at the head of the First Broad River. As early as 1835 a post office—Golden—was here. This is a view of the bottomland on the headwater of the First Broad River in Golden Valley. (Photo by James M. Walker.)

Besides monazite mining, timber, agriculture, music parks, wilderness and recreation areas, and stills, Golden Valley residents had limited opportunities until recently. People who needed employment usually had to find it outside the community until 1969. That is when Milliken opened its Golden Valley Plant. (Photo by James M. Walker.)

The Milliken Plant in Golden Valley in 1969 was the most modern circular knitting plant (at the time) in the world. (Courtesy of Milliken and Company, Spartanburg, South Carolina. Richard Dillard, director of public affairs.)

74

Important to the Golden Valley Township are its churches. This large structure is the Golden Valley First Broad Baptist Church. (Photo by James M. Walker.)

Duncan's Creek Township is bordered on the east by Cleveland County, on the north by Golden Valley Township, on the west by Logan's Store Township, and on the south by Colfax Township. The main community within Duncan's Creek Township is Hollis community. This postcard of Hollis around 1900 is a view looking west from the J.P.D. Withrow property. The postcard shows a church, a school, a store, and a livery stable. (Postcard used with permission of Frances Gettys Bailey.)

This sign across from part of the old Hollis School still welcomes the traveler to the Hollis community. (Photo by James M. Walker.)

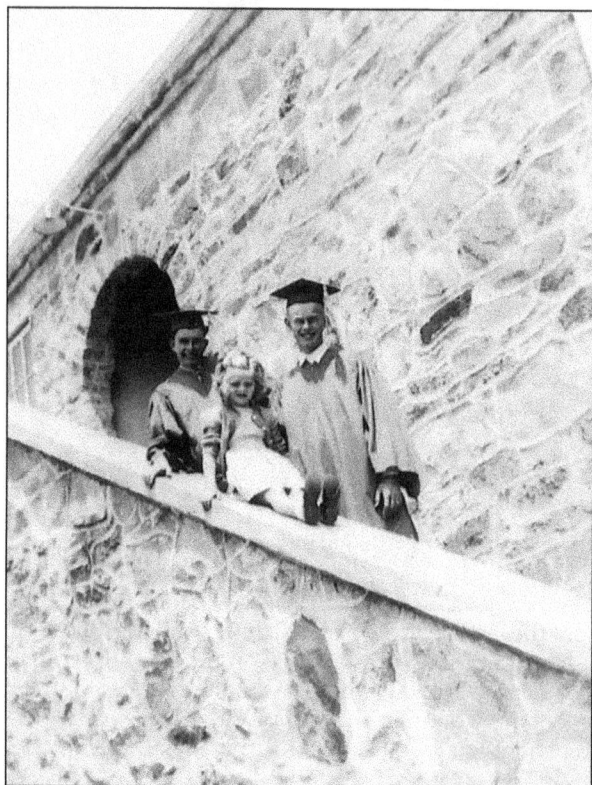

This photograph is on the steps of Hollis School in 1948. The stone masonry work is exquisite. The three people, from left to right, are Benjamin Hawkins (class of 1948), Graduation Mascot Barbara Bridges (Greene), and Dr. Worth Bridges Jr. (class of 1948). (Courtesy of Dr. Worth Bridges Jr.)

This photograph was made at the front of the Rock School House in Hollis, North Carolina, in about 1914. (Courtesy of Scott Withrow.)

Hazel Marie Green (Bridges) and Dr. Worth Bridges Jr. stand before a monument to the World War II dead from Cleveland and Rutherford County. Because of the proximity of Hollis to the Cleveland and Rutherford County line, it seemed fitting to commemorate the sacrifices of Cleveland County on one side of the marker and the sacrifices of Rutherford County on the other. (Courtesy of Dr. Worth Bridges Jr.)

The 1940 Hollis High School girls basketball team stands before the glass doors leading to the gymnasium. The players are, from left to right, Nell Waters (Edwards), Gertrude Black (Bridges), Frances McFarland, Nell Daves (Burns), Buna Daves (Edwards), Sadie Bradley, Maude Whitener, Tewie Bradley, and Inez Hunt. The photograph was in the album of Nell Daves Burns. Nell Waters Edwards gave it to her.

Withrow's Store was the center of the Hollis community for many years. Although no longer being used for sales, the store still shows its importance. (Photo by James M. Walker.)

Across the road from Withrow's store is the old post office. There is no post office assigned to Hollis today. (Photo by James M. Walker.)

The organization of Duncan's Creek Presbyterian Church took place in 1807. This brick structure is a landmark in the rural community. (Photo by James M. Walker.)

The Big Springs Baptist Church on Hollis Road is one of the few remaining institutions still operating in the Hollis community. The construction of the first log building with its dirt floor and only one room was completed around 1818. There was a second building in 1876 and a third in 1908. The fourth reached completion in 1956. (Photo by James M. Walker.)

The cemetery at Big Springs has numerous markers that dated back to the 1800s. Steve D. Price (1830–1909) and Louise E. Price (1830–1927), shown in this 1800s photo, are both interred in the cemetery. (Courtesy of Carolyn Grindstaff Barbee.)

Six

COOL SPRINGS TOWNSHIP

Cool Springs Township has Logan's Store Township to its north, Rutherfordton Township to its west, Sulphur Springs and High Shoals Townships to its south, and Colfax Township to its east. The three main locations in the Cool Springs Township include Forest City, Bostic, and Alexander Mills.

The incorporation of the town of Burnt Chimney was complete by 1877. In 1887, Burnt Chimney became Forest City in honor of Forest Davis, an area lumber merchant. A chimney-shaped marker on the public square is a reminder of the original name of the town. (Photo by James M. Walker.)

This 1908 scene in Forest City, North Carolina, shows a portion of Cherry Mountain or North Street. The church, with two front doors, was the First Presbyterian Church of Forest City. Horn's Store was the publisher of the postcard.

Forest City, N. C.   From top of Mill

This view of Forest City, North Carolina, is from the top of the mill. The Florence Mills was the publisher of this postcard from 1910.

PUBLIC SQUARE, FOREST CITY, N. C.

This early postcard of Forest City shows the public square. (Asheville Postcard Company, Asheville, North Carolina.)

FC-3 MAIN STREET AND PUBLIC SQUARE LOOKING WEST. FOREST CITY. N. C.

Forest City received an award from the U.S. Department of Agriculture in August 1927 as being one of the ten most beautiful and best-planned cities in America This early postcard (looking west) shows Main Street and the public square of Forest City. The Romina Theatre on the right side of the card was the first theatre in Rutherford County to show sound movies. On February 14, 2002, the National Register of Historic Places listed the Main Street of Forest City as a historic district. (Asheville Postcard Company, Asheville, North Carolina.)

6A442

Main Street and the public square of Forest City, North Carolina, is the scene of this postcard. The postmark for the card is 1938. (Asheville Postcard Company, Asheville, North Carolina.)

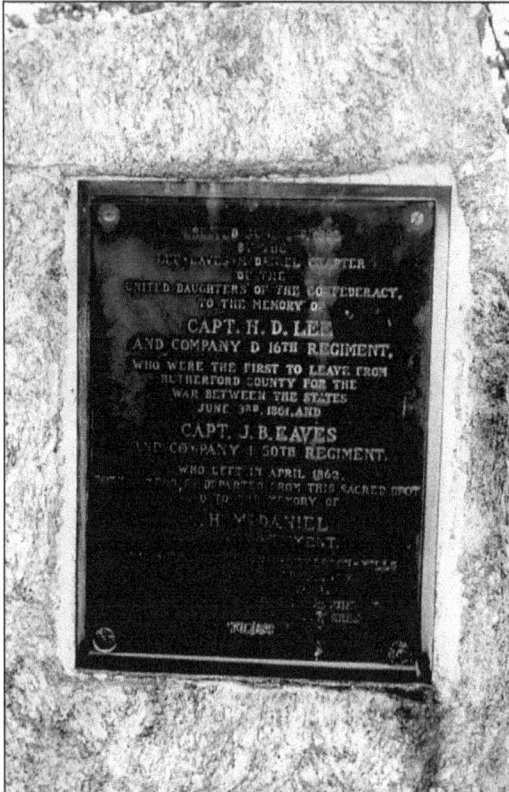

On the West Plaza of public square in Forest City is a monument marking the site of the old Burnt Chimney Muster Ground, 1861–1865. The monument was a gift from the Lee-Eaves-McDaniel Chapter of the United Daughters of the Confederacy, which was organized on March 14, 1931. (Photo by James M. Walker.)

On the public square of Main Street in Forest City is a monument to the Rutherford County World War I veterans who made the supreme sacrifice. (Photo by James M. Walker.)

IN MEMORY OF

CAPTAIN ROY HUSKEY	TROOPER R. L. "PETE" PETERSON	SERGEANT MILLARD OWEN MESSERSMITH
RUTHERFORD COUNTY SHERIFF'S DEPARTMENT	N. C. STATE HIGHWAY PATROL	RUTHERFORD COUNTY SHERIFF'S DEPARTMENT
BORN MAY 25, 1931 SHOT AND KILLED IN THE LINE OF DUTY IN RURAL RUTHERFORD COUNTY MAY 31, 1979	BORN JANUARY 29, 1942 SHOT AND KILLED IN THE LINE OF DUTY IN RURAL RUTHERFORD COUNTY MAY 31, 1979	BORN JUNE 20, 1920 SHOT AND KILLED IN THE LINE OF DUTY IN RURAL RUTHERFORD COUNTY MAY 31, 1979

"GREATER LOVE HATH NO MAN THAN THIS, THAT A MAN LAY DOWN HIS LIFE FOR HIS FRIENDS." ST. JOHN 15:13

The public square on Main Street in Forest City has one marker in honor of Capt. Roy Huskey (May 25, 1931–May 31, 1979) of the Rutherford County Sheriff's Department, Trooper R.L. Peterson (January 29, 1947–May 31,1979) of the North Carolina State Highway Patrol, and Sgt. Millard Owen Messersmith (June 20,1920–May 31, 1979). In rural Rutherford County, James Hutchins shot and killed the three men in the line of duty. (Photo by James M. Walker.)

The three officers on the marker have their story included in the movie *Rutherford County Line*, a biography of Sheriff Damon Huskey. Earl Owensby of Cliffside directed and starred in the feature. *Rutherford County Line* opened in Forest City in 1985 at the Cinema IV Theatre at the Tri-City Mall. (Courtesy of Mr. and Mrs. Damon Huskey.)

As a reminder of those from the county who gave their lives during World War II, there is now a Rutherford County Memorial Garden comprised of the bronze plaques originally placed beside the trees on Memorial Avenue. The cemetery is behind the "old" Cool Springs School on Main Street. That Memorial Garden helps to ensure that the sacrifice of the 149 men who died on duty will be remembered. (Courtesy of Roy Lewis McKain.)

Montros Jeffries, Tech 5, 585 Port Company TC, was one of two Rutherford County African Americans who gave their lives during World War II. His wife, Christine Fuller, survived him. Jeffries (January 20, 1918–July 5, 1944) is interred in the Wells Spring Church Cemetery in Forest City. Phillip Miller, the other African American, is interred in the New Hope Cemetery between Forest City and Spindale. Mr. and Mrs. Albert Miller, six brothers (George, Howard, Albert, John Thomas, Fredrick, and Julius), and sisters (Tillie, Mary, and Beulah) survived him. (Information courtesy of Barbara H. Petty and Mr. and Mrs. Milton Robinson Jr. Photo courtesy of Mr. and Mrs. Milton Robinson Jr. and Betty Jeffries.)

First Baptist Church, Forest City, N. C.

The organization of the Forest City Baptist Church was in 1825. The original name of the church was Cool Springs Baptist Church. This postcard shows the 1915 structure. (McDaniel Drug Company. Printed in Germany.)

FIRST BAPTIST CHURCH AND ALEXANDER MEMORIAL, FOREST CITY, N. C.

The facility currently in use for the Forest City Baptist Church (also known as the First Baptist Church) on 301 West Main Street in Forest City became an addition to the National Register of Historic Places in 1989. Its historic significance was the architecture of the Classical Revival style. W.E. McArthur, from Rutherfordton, published this postcard through Eagle Postcard View Company, Incorporated, New York.

FC-6 FOREST CITY ELEMENTARY SCHOOL, FOREST CITY, N. C.

Complete before the end of 1922, the brick Forest City Elementary School—just off the Old Caroleen Road—replaced the graded school built in 1903 one block north of Main Street. The school has since burned and has been replaced by a more modern brick structure on the same lot. (Asheville Postcard Company, Asheville, North Carolina.)

88

Completed in 1925, Cool Springs High School functioned for many years as the high school for Cool Springs Township. Now it serves as the administration building for Rutherford County. In 1999 it became a part of the National Register of Historic Places because of its architectural style (Classical Revival), its place in social history, and its service to education. Louis Humbert Asbury and H.A. Kistler were the architects, builders, and engineers. (Asheville Postcard Company, Asheville, North Carolina.)

In the foundation under the right front window of the U.S. Post Office in Forest City is cast the following: "Henry Morgenthau Jr., Secretary of the Treasury. James A. Fairly, Postmaster General. 1937." Mr. W.H. McArthur of Forest City found the information on the post office foundation (now used as a chiropractic clinic) and transcribed it for the author. (Postcard is from Asheville Postcard Company, Asheville, North Carolina.)

A prominent mural is evident to the traveler going west on Main Street. This mural was the work of Clive Haynes. The mural shows a view of Main Street as the scene would appear if one were traveling east. (Photo by James M. Walker.)

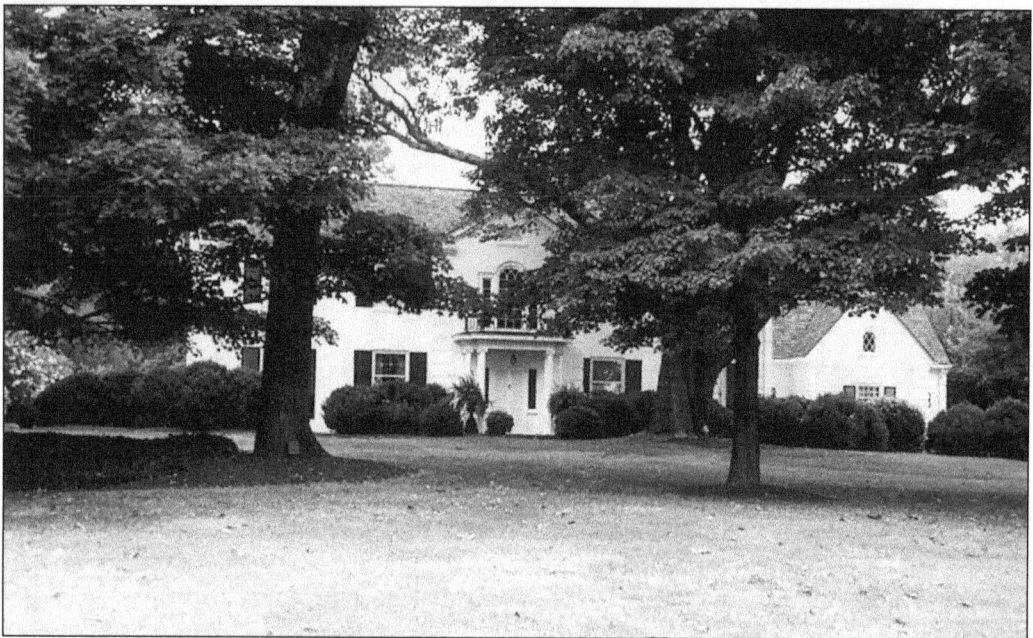

On October 15, 2001, the T. Max Watson House on 297 East Main Street in Forest City became a part of the National Register of Historic Places. Watson served Rutherford County as general manager of the Sterling Hosiery Mills in Spindale, county commissioner, a member of the State Highway Commission as appointed by Gov. Clyde R. Hoey, and director of the First Industrial Bank at Forest City and Rutherfordton. (Photo by James M. Walker.)

The James Dexter Ledbetter House (building #82003511) became a part of the National Register of Historic Places in 1982. Except for its material of construction, the house is identical to the Washburn House (also in the National Register of Historic Places as of February 20, 2002) in Logan's Store Township. The house is located on U.S. Highway 74. Construction of the single-dwelling home representing both the Colonial Revival and the Classical Revival styles was complete in 1914. Robert Ewart Burns, an electrical engineer from Ellenboro and one of the first employees of the Cliffside Steam Station of Duke Power, upgraded the electrical wiring in the home in later years. (Photo by James M. Walker.)

These Civilian Conservation Corps enrollees are learning to become excellent cooks and bakers. They are members of Company 5423 and are working in Forest City. (Courtesy of New Deal Network, http://newdeal.feri.org/library/c07a.htm.)

This postcard shows Lake Forest Camp, Forest City, North Carolina.

This postcard depicts Reinhardt Park in Forest City. The postmark is 1941.

This image shows the Forest City depot, which no longer exists. (Courtesy of W.H. McArthur.)

The town of Bostic is between the Second Broad River and Puzzle Creek. This photograph shows the laying of the rails in Bostic, North Carolina, in 1913. J.L. Culbreth supervises the work. The location of the rails was one factor that led to the establishment of the Bostic Brickyard. (Used by permission of James M. Walker.)

A major industry in the Bostic area was the Bostic Brickyard that operated from 1919 until the 1960s. The Bostic location was ideal; it had the train yard on one side and the Second Broad River with a supply of clay on the other. This image shows the kilns used for baking the bricks. (Photo by James M. Walker.)

These supply sheds are evidence of the importance at one time of the brick industry to Bostic and the surrounding community. (Photo by James M. Walker.)

Alexander Mills was incorporated in 1915. It received its name for a textile mill established by J.F. Alexander. An interesting feature there is the Globe Theatre. (Photo by James M. Walker.)

This is a photograph of Grindstaff's Furniture Store, which was in Forest City. Now known as Grindstaff's Interiors, the store has changed dramatically in the past half century in size and exterior design. Grindstaff's had the largest stock of quality furniture in the Southeast (1966) and had the largest display of fine furniture in the Carolinas (1964). (Courtesy of Boyce F. Grindstaff.)

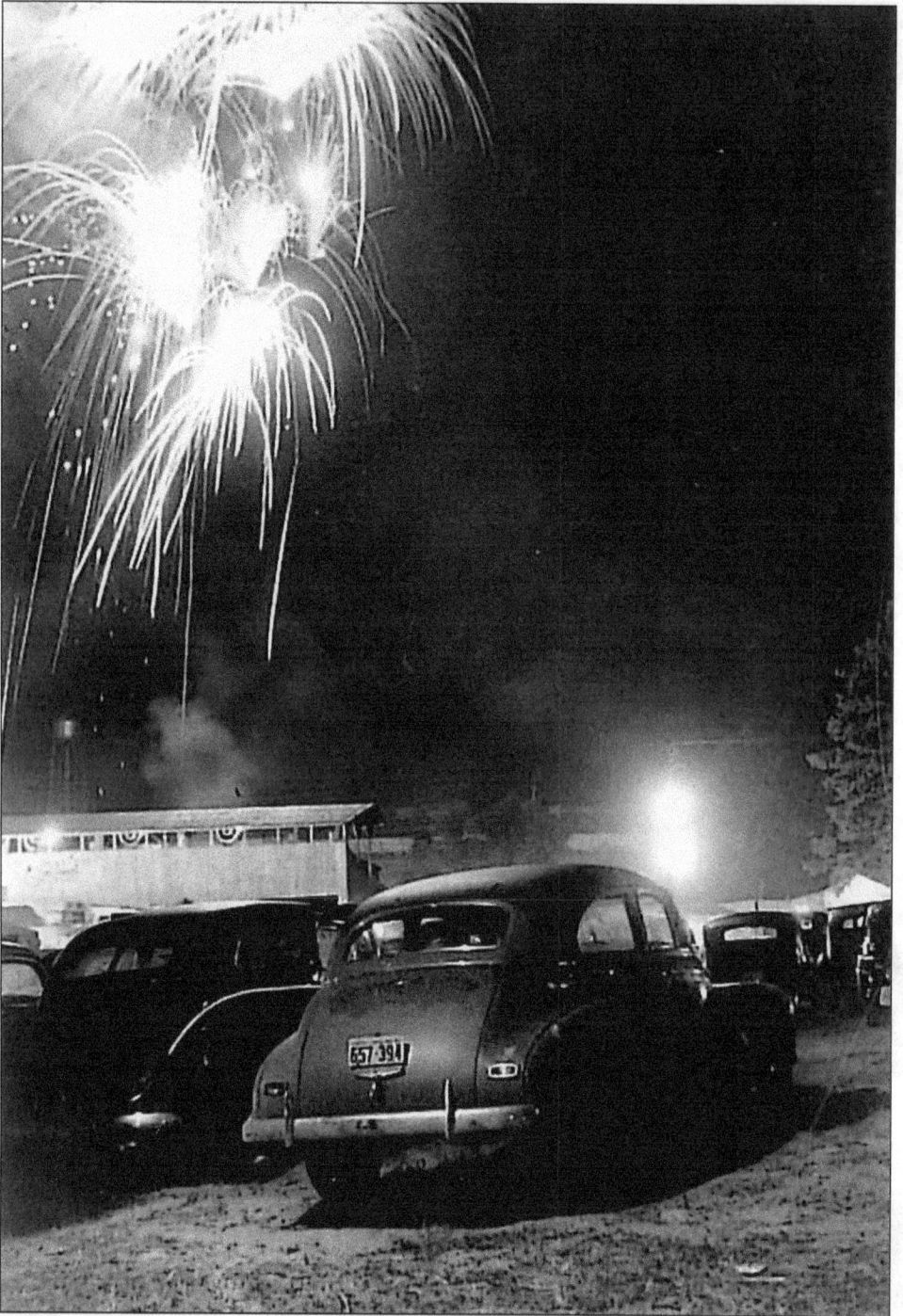

Each fall, about the time that most Rutherford County farmers had their first bale of cotton for spending money, Rutherford County held its county fair. In addition to exhibits, concessions, and agricultural displays, traveling rides arrived to attract even more visitors. The fairgrounds between Forest City and Spindale provided the location for the annual event. (Courtesy of W.H. McArthur.)

Seven

HIGH SHOALS TOWNSHIP

The High Shoals Township is the most southeastern of the townships in Rutherford County. Its border to the east is Cleveland County; its border to the west is Sulphur Springs Township. South Carolina forms its southern border and two townships, Cool Springs and Colfax Townships, form the northern border. Within its borders are four main towns: Caroleen, Avondale, Henrietta, and Cliffside.

The existence of Caroleen, Avondale, Henrietta, and Cliffside is in large part due to the work of Raleigh Rutherford Haynes, the oldest son born June 30, 1851, to Sarah Walker Haynes and Charles Hodge Haynes. Raleigh Rutherford Haynes was born in the Ferry community of Rutherford County in 1851, and his father died when he was seven. The house in which he was born was a log structure, which was covered with weather boarding. Janice Bridges Swing, his great-granddaughter, moved the home to Cliffside Estates in Cliffside, removed the weatherboarding, and restored the log structure. (Photograph by permission of Janice Swing and made by Grover C. Haynes Jr.)

This photograph of Raleigh Rutherford Haynes is from the files of Mrs. Hazel Haynes Bridges and is used courtesy of Mrs. Bridges and Mr. Grover C. Haynes Jr.

Amanda Loretta Carpenter and Raleigh Rutherford Haynes had eight children before her death on February 2, 1890. This photograph on Christmas Day 1916 shows R.R. Haynes and children. From left to right are R.R. Haynes (June 30, 1851–February 6, 1917), Mrs. Florence Haynes Jenkins, Robert E. Haynes, Charles H. Haynes, Mrs. Sara Haynes Love, Walter H. Haynes, Grover C. Haynes, Mrs. Eula Haynes Shull, and Mrs. Virginia Haynes Caldwell. (Page 57 of *Raleigh Rutherford Haynes* by Mrs. Grover C. Haynes Sr., Miller Printing Company, Asheville, North Carolina, 1954, and used by permission of Grover C. Haynes Jr.)

Ina Fortune Haynes, wife of Grover C. Haynes Sr., was born on November 28, 1888 and died on December 20, 1963. She collected information on the Haynes family and on the achievements of Raleigh Rutherford Haynes, in particular. She authored the book *Raleigh Rutherford Haynes*, published by Miller Printing Company in Asheville, North Carolina, 1954. (Courtesy of Grover C. Haynes Jr.)

Raleigh Rutherford Haynes began buying land in High Shoals in 1885. He and the other stockholders began clearing the land and constructing a mill in Henrietta with homes for the workers in 1887. Another mill was built in 1895 that was named Caroleen Mills after stockholder S.B. Tanner's mother Caroline. In 1896 Haynes built a home in Henrietta where he and his children lived until he built the home in Cliffside. (Page 22 of *Raleigh Rutherford Haynes* by Mrs. Grover C. Haynes Sr., Miller Printing Company, Asheville, North Carolina, 1954, and used by permission of Grover C. Haynes Jr.)

Avondale Mills was the name of the second mill at Henrietta. (Page 48 of *Raleigh Rutherford Haynes* by Mrs. Grover C. Haynes Sr., Miller Printing Company, Asheville, North Carolina, 1954, and used by permission of Grover C. Haynes Jr.)

This store at Henrietta (now Avondale) that Raleigh Rutherford Haynes built about 1895 became the Haynes Brick Store. (Page 61 of *Raleigh Rutherford Haynes* by Mrs. Grover C. Haynes Sr., Miller Printing Company, Asheville, North Carolina, 1954, and used by permission of Grover C. Haynes Jr.)

100

A second store at West Henrietta (now Avondale) that Raleigh Rutherford Haynes built became the Haynes Store Number 2. It was a frame building. (Page 62 of *Raleigh Rutherford Haynes* by Mrs. Grover C. Haynes Sr., Miller Printing Company, Asheville, North Carolina, 1954, and used by permission of Grover C. Haynes Jr.)

Several Cliffside workers move a large drum down an unpaved Cliffside street. Notice the mill houses in the background, which the mill owners offered to workers for rent. (The photograph is courtesy of Colleen Biggerstaff.)

This scene is at the cotton warehouses in Cliffside soon after the beginning of its operation. (Page 74 of *Raleigh Rutherford Haynes* by Mrs. Grover C. Haynes Sr., Miller Printing Company, Asheville, North Carolina, 1954, and used by permission of Grover C. Haynes Jr.)

In 1902, Raleigh Rutherford Haynes built a home in Cliffside. (Page 23 of *Raleigh Rutherford Haynes* by Mrs. Grover C. Haynes Sr., Miller Printing Company, Asheville, North Carolina, 1954, and used by permission of Grover C. Haynes Jr.)

This is the first home of the Haynes Bank, which Raleigh Rutherford Haynes established in Henrietta (now Avondale) in 1907. During the Great Depression this was one of only five in the county to survive. (Page 89 of *Raleigh Rutherford Haynes* by Mrs. Grover C. Haynes Sr., Miller Printing Company, Asheville, North Carolina, 1954, and used by permission of Grover C. Haynes Jr.)

This is a view of the town square in Cliffside in 1913. (Page 77 of *Raleigh Rutherford Haynes* by Mrs. Grover C. Haynes Sr., Miller Printing Company, Asheville, North Carolina, 1954, and used by permission of Grover C. Haynes Jr.)

This engine and coach were used on the Cliffside Railroad. They were originally part of the elevated railways in New York City in the 1890s. (Page 79 of *Raleigh Rutherford Haynes* by Mrs. Grover C. Haynes Sr., Miller Printing Company, Asheville, North Carolina, 1954, and used by permission of Grover C. Haynes Jr.)

The area for education in Cliffside was in the mill itself, over the Mill Store, and later in its own building. This shows the first school building in Cliffside. (Page 45 of *Raleigh Rutherford Haynes* by Mrs. Grover C. Haynes Sr., Miller Printing Company, Asheville, North Carolina, 1954, and used by permission of Grover C. Haynes Jr.)

CLIFFSIDE PUBLIC SCHOOL BUILDING, CLIFFSIDE, N. C.

When the wooden structure grew too small, Cliffside could boast a new brick school building by 1922. Cliffside School with its Classical-Revival style became an addition to the National Register of Historic Places in 1998. (Curteich-Chicago "C. T. Art-Colortone" Postcard.)

In 1940, the Duke Power Steam Station at Cliffside began operation. (Photograph courtesy of Duke Energy Corporation.)

Many of the employees lived in the Duke Power Village constructed for them. This aerial view of the village shows the streets and houses. (Courtesy of Duke Energy Corporation.)

At 10 years of age, Cliffside resident Earl Owensby became fascinated with films when he worked as an usher at the Cliffside Theater. A former marine, he later became a successful entrepreneur and founder of several successful companies, primarily in the industrial supply business. He produced and starred in his first feature film *Challenge* and used the profits to construct his own film studio near Shelby, North Carolina. Owensby also purchased an uncompleted nuclear power plant that became a setting for several films, including *The Abyss*. This publicity photograph appeared in the 1980s about the time of the release of *Rutherford County Line*; the biographical movie is a tribute to Damon Huskey, the sheriff of Rutherford County for 24 years—almost a quarter of a century. (Courtesy of Nell Price Burns and Robert Eric Davis.)

This photograph shows the Presbyterian Church of Cliffside, which is no longer there, and a house in background, which was a home for teachers. (Page 41 of *Raleigh Rutherford Haynes* by Mrs. Grover C. Haynes Sr., Miller Printing Company, Asheville, North Carolina, 1954, and used by permission of Grover C. Haynes Jr.)

This is a 1950s view of the Avondale Methodist Church at Avondale. (Page 42 of *Raleigh Rutherford Haynes* by Mrs. Grover C. Haynes Sr., Miller Printing Company, Asheville, North Carolina, 1954, and used by permission of Grover C. Haynes Jr.)

Pausing for a photograph, from left to right, are (front) Roy Biggerstaff; and (back) Clemmer Thomas holding Ann Thomas (Billingsley), Odell Biggerstaff, and Virgil Biggerstaff. (Photograph made by Frances Biggerstaff and courtesy of Colleen Biggerstaff.)

This 1950s photograph shows the Cliffside Baptist Church. The steps in front often appear in the photographs of many weddings. (Page 43 of *Raleigh Rutherford Haynes* by Mrs. Grover C. Haynes Sr., Miller Printing Company, Asheville, North Carolina, 1954, and used by permission of Grover C. Haynes Jr.)

Before integration, the Haynes Grove Chapel was the Baptist Church for African Americans in Cliffside. (Page 44 of *Raleigh Rutherford Haynes* by Mrs. Grover C. Haynes Sr., Miller Printing Company, Asheville, North Carolina, 1954, and used by permission of Grover C. Haynes Jr.)

The old Simmons School House in the Ferry community was the gathering place for the 1953 reunion of some of the students. (Page 63 of *Raleigh Rutherford Haynes* by Mrs. Grover C. Haynes Sr., Miller Printing Company, Asheville, North Carolina, 1954, and used by permission of Grover C. Haynes Jr.)

A business in Cliffside that seems to have withstood the test of time is McKinney's (now McKinney-Landreth) Funeral Home. A.C. McKinney began the business in 1953. Horton and Jerene Landreth have been serving the community recently in a new brick building. Many residents still remember the older white frame structure, which housed the business that has remained locally owned and locally operated. (Courtesy of Horton Landreth.)

Three workers of the Cliffside Railroad pause for the camera. (Courtesy Colleen Biggerstaff.)

World War II was a great blight on Rutherford County; over 5,000 men from the county (12% of the population) took part in the war. Tri-High School truly gave sacrificially. Seventeen young men from Tri-High School, which served Avondale, Henrietta, and Caroleen, died in the service of their country.

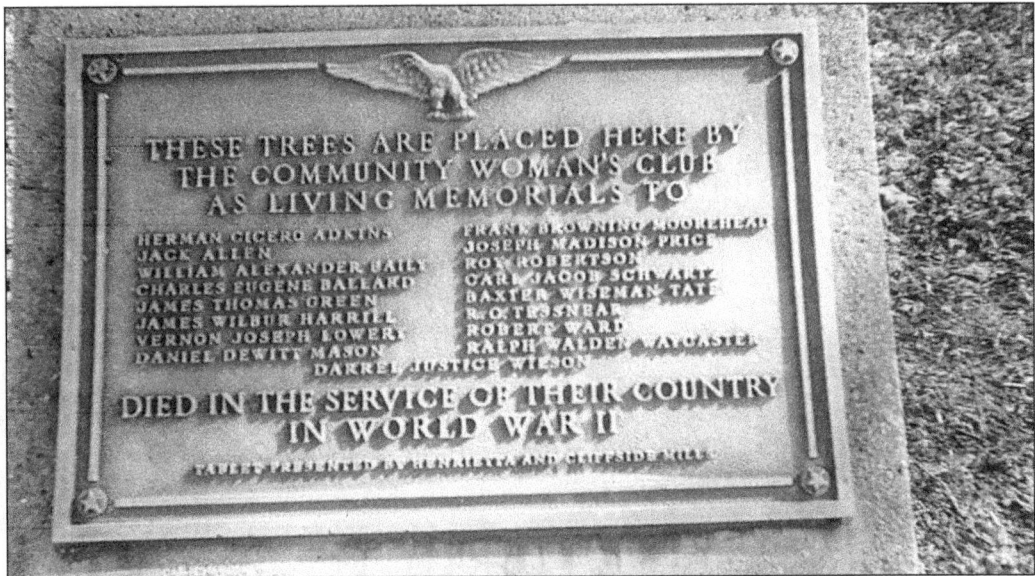

A marker to the memory of the Tri-High Students who made the supreme sacrifice is at the original site of that school, now the Thomas Jefferson Charter School on Highway 221-A and near Cliffside. The ones who died were Herman Cicero Adkins, Jack Allen, William Alexander Bailey, Charles Eugene Ballard, James Thomas Green, James Wilbur Harrill, Vernon Joseph Lowery, Daniel Dewitt Mason, Frank Browning Morehead, Joseph Madison Price, Roy Robertson, Carl Jacob Schwartz, Baxter Wiseman Tate, R.O. Tessnear, Robert Ward, Ralph Walden Waycaster, and Darrel Justice Wilson. (Tri-High Marker.)

BIRD'S EYE VIEW OF CLIFFSDE, N. C.

This bird's-eye view of Cliffside shows a peaceful, neat area for residents. (Courtesy of Anne and

CLIFFSIDE MILLS AND LAKE SHOWING FALLS, CLIFFSIDE, N. C.

This early postcard shows Cliffside Mills, the lake, and falls. (Courtesy of Anne and Paula

Paula Cargill. Postcard by C.T. American Art, Chicago, Illinois, R89682.)

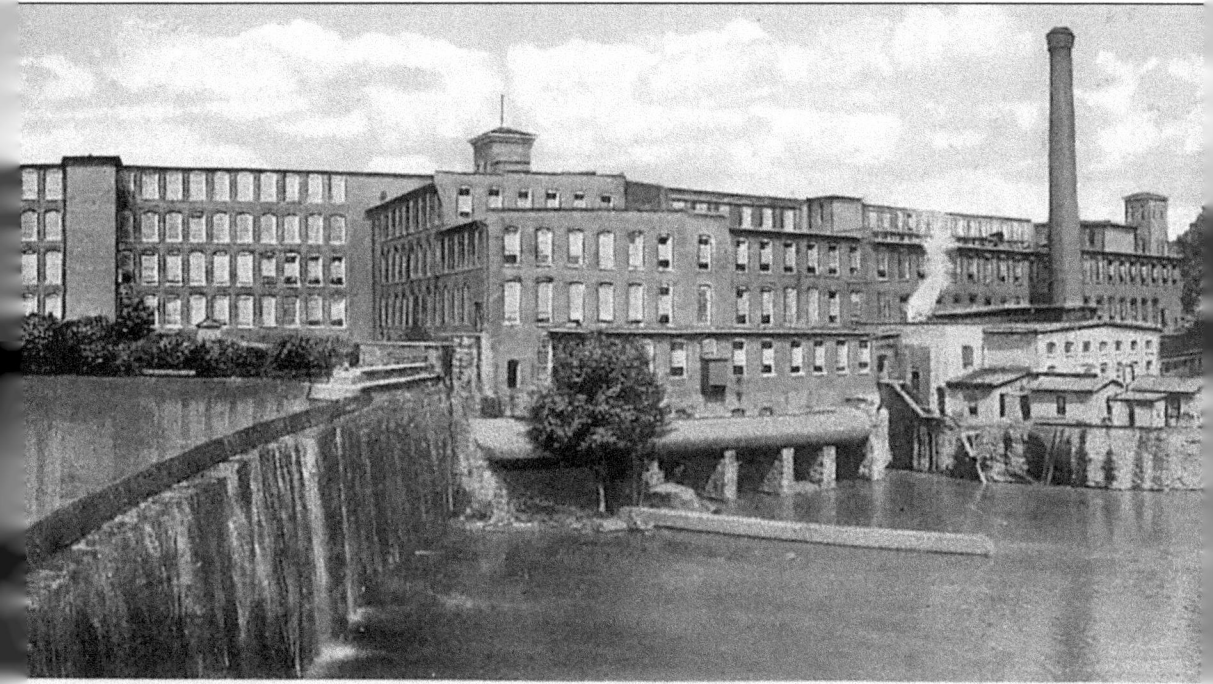

Cargill. Postcard by C.T. American Art, Chicago, Illinois, R89682.)

This early picture postcard shows the Cliffside Mills Store and the R.R. Haynes Memorial Building in Cliffside. The R.R. Haynes Memorial Building, which housed the Cliffside Theatre, was a tribute to Haynes by his son Charles. The dedication of the building to the Cliffside

This early picture postcard shows a view of Cliffside, looking north from the square. The Cliffside Mills Store and the R.R. Haynes Memorial Building are on the left. (Courtesy of Anne

citizens was on June 24, 1922. (Courtesy of Anne and Paula Cargill. Postcard by C.T. American Art, Chicago, Illinois, R89682.)

and Paula Cargill. Postcard by C.T. American Art, Chicago, Illinois, R89682.)

This is a view of the lobby of the R.R. Haynes Memorial Building in Cliffside. (C.T. American Art, Chicago, Illinois, R89682.)

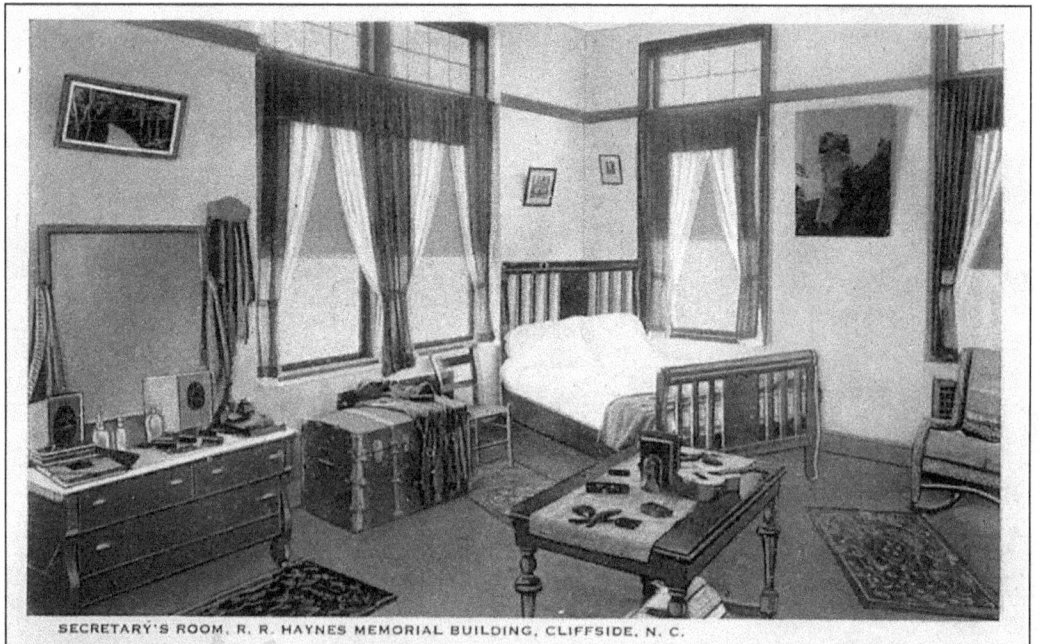

This is a view of the secretary's room in the R.R. Haynes Memorial Building in Cliffside. (C.T. American Art, Chicago, Illinois, R89682.)

Eight

COLFAX TOWNSHIP

Formed in 1868 after the establishment of most of the other townships in Rutherford County, Colfax Township received its name from Schuyler Colfax, who was vice president from 1869 to 1873. The eastern boundary of Colfax Township is Cleveland County. Duncan's Creek Township and Logan's Store Township lie to the north. Cool Springs Township borders Colfax Township on the west, while High Shoals Township lies to the south/southeast. Important places within the Colfax Township include the Washburn (Washburn's Store) community, the Hopewell community (named for the local church), and Ellenboro.

Washburn (formerly Green's Grove) is between Puzzle and Heaveners Creek. Lexine was the name of the 1901–1905 post office. The name came from Lexine Pruett, the daughter of Greenbury Pruett, who was a member of the general assembly. Washburn's Store, part of the historic district listed in the National Register of Historic Places, is located at the line between Colfax Township and Logan's Store Township. (Photo by James M. Walker.)

The Washburn Historic District, which includes the Washburn House, became a part of the National Register of Historic Places on February 20, 2002. Except for its material of construction, the house is identical to the Ledbetter House (also in the National Register of Historic Places) in Cool Springs Township. This house is of red brick while the Ledbetter House is snowy white in appearance. The construction of the single dwelling home that represents both the Colonial Revival and the Classical Revival styles was complete in 1914. (Photo by James M. Walker.)

Hopewell community received its name from Hopewell Methodist Church, which was established in 1800 and became the second oldest Methodist Church in Rutherford County. (Oak Grove Methodist Church, established in 1792, is the oldest.) The current building was completed in the late 1940s. (Photo by James M. Walker.)

118

Although no longer in operation, the Hopewell Gin served cotton farmers in the Hopewell area for many years. (Photo by James M. Walker.)

In 1874, Ellenboro possibly received its name from Ellen Robinson, the terminally-ill daughter of a Carolina Central Railroad engineer. On one of his trips from Hamlet he heard the area was looking for a name and said that he would donate a bell if they used his daughter's name. Another story is that the names of Burwell Blanton Byars, the owner of much land, and his wife were combined to make the name Ellenburwell, which later became Ellenboro. The setting of the corporate limits of Ellenboro was on February 28, 1889. The limits (in relation to the Carolina Central Depot—later the old Seaboard Airline Railway Depot) were a half-mile in any direction from the depot. (Photo by James M. Walker.)

Ellenboro's three-room school housed grades one through eleven in the 1910s and early 1920s. Students moved into the new brick school in 1924, and the school became a residence. Anita Price Davis's parents rented an apartment on the second floor for a while before her birth. (Courtesy of James M. Walker.)

Originally constructed in 1924, the three-floor, brick Ellenboro School housed local students from first grade through graduation for 36 years. For more than 40 additional years, the facility was used as an elementary school. The auditorium was added in 1932. Several other additions helped provide the facilities that the students and community needed. The lunchroom was the site of vaccinations for the community, bazaars for local churches, and ice cream socials. A new cafeteria was added in 1957. (Courtesy of Principal Frank Wall, Ellenboro School.)

In 1931, Ellenboro High School was Class B Champions in Rutherford County. The players were, from left to right, (front row) Norris Callahan, Ervin Smart, Lloyd Greene, Vernon Allen, and Wayne Smart; (middle row) Gold Allen, Carl McKinney, Miles Jones, and J.L. Hamrick; (back row) Curtis Price (principal), James Walker (manager), and Louis Nanney Sr. (coach). (Courtesy of James M. Walker.)

A.B. Bushong, agriculture teacher at Ellenboro School, instituted the sweet potato crop in the area to provide a cash crop, started a chick hatchery with a 7,000- egg capacity, organized a cannery, taught agriculture classes for adults, served as chief observer of the aircraft warning post in Ellenboro during World War II, provided training for returning veterans, organized tours for members of the community, organized the installation and painting of 600 mailboxes, and served as agriculture advisor to residents. (Courtesy of Principal Frank Wall, Ellenboro School.)

In the fall of the year when the cotton harvest had begun, farmers set up their agricultural exhibits, school children set up their displays, and the traveling workers set up their amusement rides for the Colfax Free Fair (later the Ellenboro Fair). Begun as an annual event for the locals, the Colfax Free Fair (started by A.B. Bushong in 1929) on occasion had its attendees elect Miss Colfax Free Fair. The 1958 Miss Colfax Free Fair was Bonnie Hamrick, center, with flowers. Her attendants, pictured from left to right, were Sybil Sellars, Linda Butler (past Queen), Anna Walker (Greenway), and Carol Newton (Mitchem). (Courtesy of Anna Walker Greenway.)

Many schoolchildren bought school supplies and snacks at Doss Martin's Store—just across the road from the school. Classes in home economics bought their groceries for preparing foods, and even needles and thread, at his store. (Photo by James M. Walker.)

Plato Rollins Price's stores at the Rutherford and Cleveland County line were early 1940 precursors of the shopping mall. In one area, he built a service station, grocery store, restaurant, hardware store, department store, and antique shop. E.W. and Bill Robbins managed the Gulf Service Station and grocery store. The store was "one-stop shopping with" meats, hoop cheese, salt fish in a keg, oil, tires, batteries, and a mechanic on duty. Sometimes the train would stop to get bologna, cheese, and crackers. Eules Cartee and Bill Robbins are shown in the photo. (Courtesy of Mr. and Mrs. Bill Robbins.)

This side shot of the County Line Service Station shows Bill Robbins's 1940 Ford Coupe and Tommy Robbins's 1946 Ford Sedan. (Courtesy of Mr. and Mrs. Bill Robbins.)

Carolyn Grindstaff Barbee bought the Dairi-O and Grill from her grandfather, P.R. Price. Her menu included sandwiches, fries, shakes, and fried pies with ice cream. Curb service was an amenity. (Courtesy of Carolyn Grindstaff Barbee.)

In 1945, Chess McCartney, "The Goat Man," from Jeffersonville, Georgia, drove his goat-drawn wagon through Ellenboro and stopped at Price's Store at the county line, a regular stop for him when he was in the area. Plato Rollins Price secured a ride on the wagon for himself and his granddaughter Anita Price (Davis). Mr. McCartney helped finance his moves through the county by selling postcards of himself. In the course of his 30 years on the road, Mr. McCartney (1901–1998) traveled all the way to California, to Ohio, and to every state in the United States but Hawaii.

Mr. McCartney went to the Eastview Nursing Home in Georgia. Anita Price Davis visited him in 1991. They discussed his visits to Price's Store when he was in Rutherford County, North Carolina.

Many Rutherford County radios were tuned each day to WBT-Charlotte (the first radio station in the state), WBBO (the first radio station in the county), and WAGY (the second Rutherford County station). Jerrell Bedford, an Ellenboro High School graduate, became the radio personality "Pappy" when he sat down before the microphone at WAGY. Pappy stands here with Loretta Lynn. After many years in broadcasting, Bedford is semi-retired. (Courtesy of Jerrell Bedford.)

Mary Fredrick (Thompson) grew up in Ellenboro and received her education in the Rutherford County Schools. She graduated from Carver High School and earned her CNA License from Isothermal Community College. She married Thomas C. Thompson on June 2, 1956. The couple helped in the management of Thompson's Rest Home (the first rest home for African Americans in Rutherford County) and Thompson Brothers' Funeral Home. When Flori Roberts cosmetics for blacks came into the county, Mary was the model for the makeup. (Courtesy of James R. Brown, publisher of *The Daily Courier*.)

The Colfax Gin built in the 1920s is still important to the Colfax Township. (Photo by James M. Walker.)

Van Harrill's General Store was a feature of Ellenboro for many years. J.L. Culbreth kept the books for the store. These accounting pages indicate some of the prices of the period. Records are courtesy of James M. Walker.

The Woman's Club in Ellenboro provided a clubhouse for meetings, family gatherings, and many events. Located on Highway 74, the white frame building still stands. (Photo by James M. Walker.)

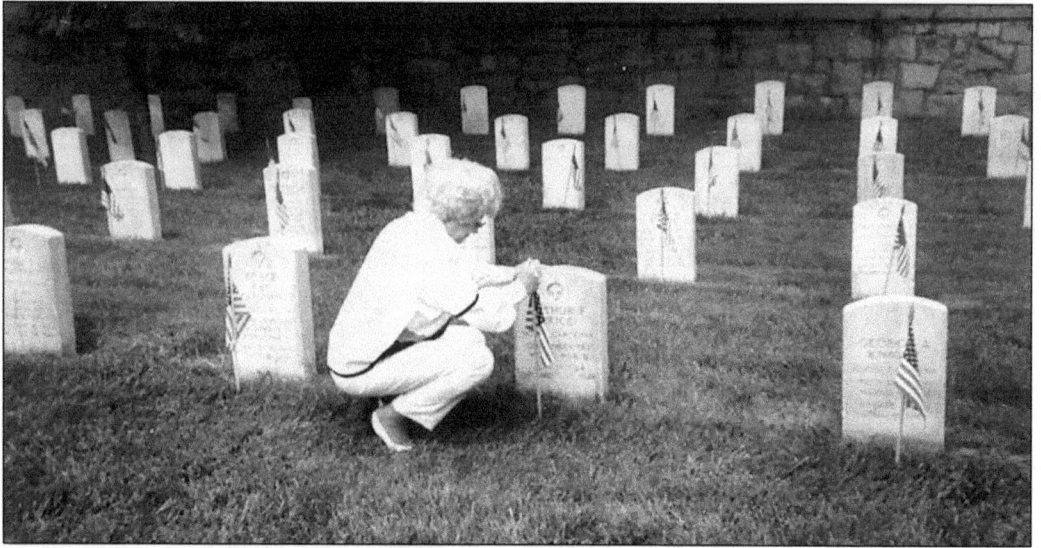

Rutherford County always did its part during wartime. Participation in World War II was no exception. Ten men from Ellenboro made the supreme sacrifice. After the war some families asked the government to bring their family member to a local cemetery; other families preferred that their loved one remain undisturbed wherever they were resting. The family of one Ellenboro soldier chose a third option. The remains of Pfc. Arthur Fred Price are now in the National Cemetery in Salisbury, North Carolina. Nell Price Burns visited his grave regularly. This visit was on Memorial Day in 1990.

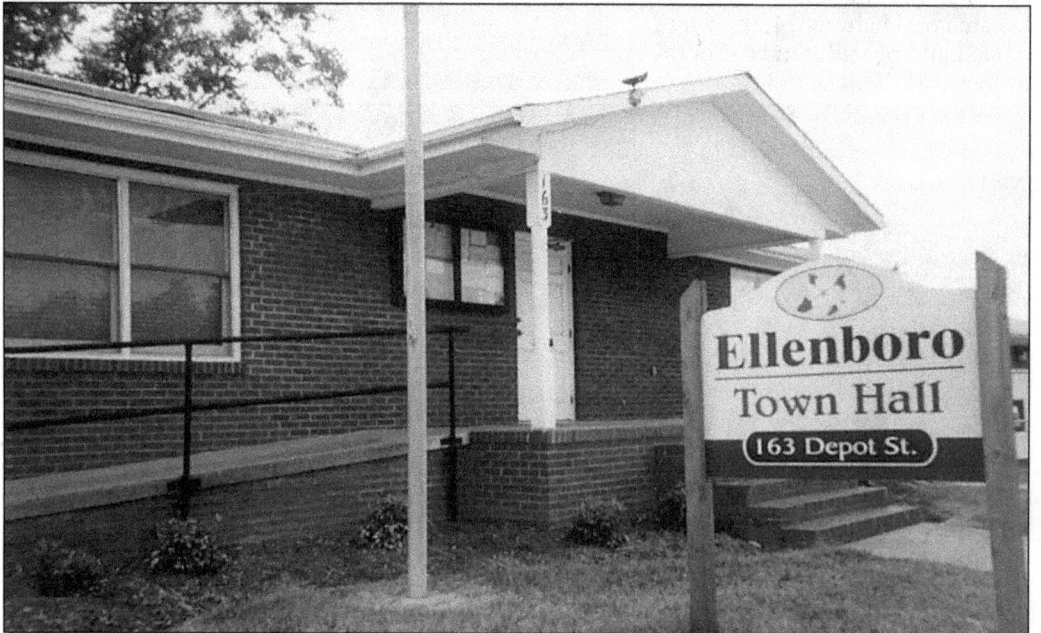

The Piedmont House, across the road from the Carolina Central/Seaboard Railroad Depot, was one of the two boarding houses in Ellenboro. Sarah Harrill Martin and her family ran the boarding house for several decades to supplement the family income. In 1976, the town bought the Piedmont House from the Martin family and constructed the town hall on the site. (Photo by James M. Walker.)

Visit us at
arcadiapublishing.com

www.ingramcontent.com/pod-product-compliance
Lightning Source LLC
Chambersburg PA
CBHW080611110426

42813CB00006B/1471